Managed UEM
Complete Self-Assessment Guide

The guidance in this Self-Assessment is bas
practices and standards in business process architecture, design and
quality management. The guidance is also based on the professional
judgment of the individual collaborators listed in the Acknowledgments.

Notice of rights

Trademarks

Table of Contents

About The Art of Service

The Art of Service, Business Process Architects since 2000, is dedicated to helping stakeholders achieve excellence.

Defining, designing, creating, and implementing a process to solve a stakeholders challenge or meet an objective is the most valuable role... In EVERY group, company, organization and department.

Unless you're talking a one-time, single-use project, there should be a process. Whether that process is managed and implemented by humans, AI, or a combination of the two, it needs to be designed by someone with a complex enough perspective to ask the right questions.

Someone capable of asking the right questions and step back and say, 'What are we really trying to accomplish here? And is there a different way to look at it?'

With The Art of Service's Standard Requirements Self-Assessments, we empower people who can do just that — whether their title is marketer, entrepreneur, manager, salesperson, consultant, Business Process Manager, executive assistant, IT Manager, CIO etc... —they are the people who rule the future. They are people who watch the process as it happens, and ask the right questions to make the process work better.

Contact us when you need any support with this Self-Assessment and any help with templates, blue-prints and examples of standard documents you might need:

http://theartofservice.com
service@theartofservice.com

Acknowledgments

This checklist was developed under the auspices of The Art of Service, chaired by Gerardus Blokdyk.

Representatives from several client companies participated in the preparation of this Self-Assessment.

In addition, we are thankful for the design and printing services provided.

Included Resources - how to access

Included with your purchase of the book is the Managed UEM Self-Assessment Spreadsheet Dashboard which contains all questions and Self-Assessment areas and auto-generates insights, graphs, and project RACI planning - all with examples to get you started right away.

How? Simply send an email to
access@theartofservice.com
with this books' title in the subject to get the Managed UEM Self Assessment Tool right away.

You will receive the following contents with New and Updated specific criteria:

- The latest quick edition of the book in PDF

- The latest complete edition of the book in PDF, which criteria correspond to the criteria in...

- The Self-Assessment Excel Dashboard, and...

- Example pre-filled Self-Assessment Excel Dashboard to get familiar with results generation

- In-depth specific Checklists covering the topic

- Project management checklists and templates to assist with implementation

INCLUDES LIFETIME SELF ASSESSMENT UPDATES

Every self assessment comes with Lifetime Updates and Lifetime Free Updated Books. Lifetime Updates is an industry-first feature which allows you to receive verified self assessment updates, ensuring you always have the most accurate information at your fingertips.

Get it now- you will be glad you did - do it now, before you forget.

Send an email to **access@theartofservice.com** with this books' title in the subject to get the Managed UEM Self Assessment Tool right away.

Your feedback is invaluable to us

If you recently bought this book, we would love to hear from you! You can do this by writing a review on amazon (or the online store where you purchased this book) about your last purchase! As part of our continual service improvement process, we love to hear real client experiences and feedback.

How does it work?
To post a review on Amazon, just log in to your account and click on the Create Your Own Review button (under Customer Reviews) of the relevant product page. You can find examples of product reviews in Amazon. If you purchased from another online store, simply follow their procedures.

What happens when I submit my review?
Once you have submitted your review, send us an email at review@theartofservice.com with the link to your review so we can properly thank you for your feedback.

Purpose of this Self-Assessment

This Self-Assessment has been developed to improve understanding of the requirements and elements of Managed UEM, based on best practices and standards in business process architecture, design and quality management.

It is designed to allow for a rapid Self-Assessment to determine how closely existing management practices and procedures correspond to the elements of the Self-Assessment.

The criteria of requirements and elements of Managed UEM have been rephrased in the format of a Self-Assessment questionnaire, with a seven-criterion scoring system, as explained in this document.

In this format, even with limited background knowledge of

Managed UEM, a manager can quickly review existing operations to determine how they measure up to the standards. This in turn can serve as the starting point of a 'gap analysis' to identify management tools or system elements that might usefully be implemented in the organization to help improve overall performance.

How to use the Self-Assessment

On the following pages are a series of questions to identify to what extent your Managed UEM initiative is complete in comparison to the requirements set in standards.

To facilitate answering the questions, there is a space in front of each question to enter a score on a scale of '1' to '5'.

1 Strongly Disagree

2 Disagree

3 Neutral

4 Agree

5 Strongly Agree

Read the question and rate it with the following in front of mind:

'In my belief,
the answer to this question is clearly defined'.

There are two ways in which you can choose to interpret this statement;
1. how aware are you that the answer to the question is clearly defined
2. for more in-depth analysis you can choose to gather

evidence and confirm the answer to the question. This obviously will take more time, most Self-Assessment users opt for the first way to interpret the question and dig deeper later on based on the outcome of the overall Self-Assessment.

A score of '1' would mean that the answer is not clear at all, where a '5' would mean the answer is crystal clear and defined. Leave emtpy when the question is not applicable or you don't want to answer it, you can skip it without affecting your score. Write your score in the space provided.

After you have responded to all the appropriate statements in each section, compute your average score for that section, using the formula provided, and round to the nearest tenth. Then transfer to the corresponding spoke in the Managed UEM Scorecard on the second next page of the Self-Assessment.

Your completed Managed UEM Scorecard will give you a clear presentation of which Managed UEM areas need attention.

Managed UEM Scorecard Example

Example of how the finalized Scorecard can look like:

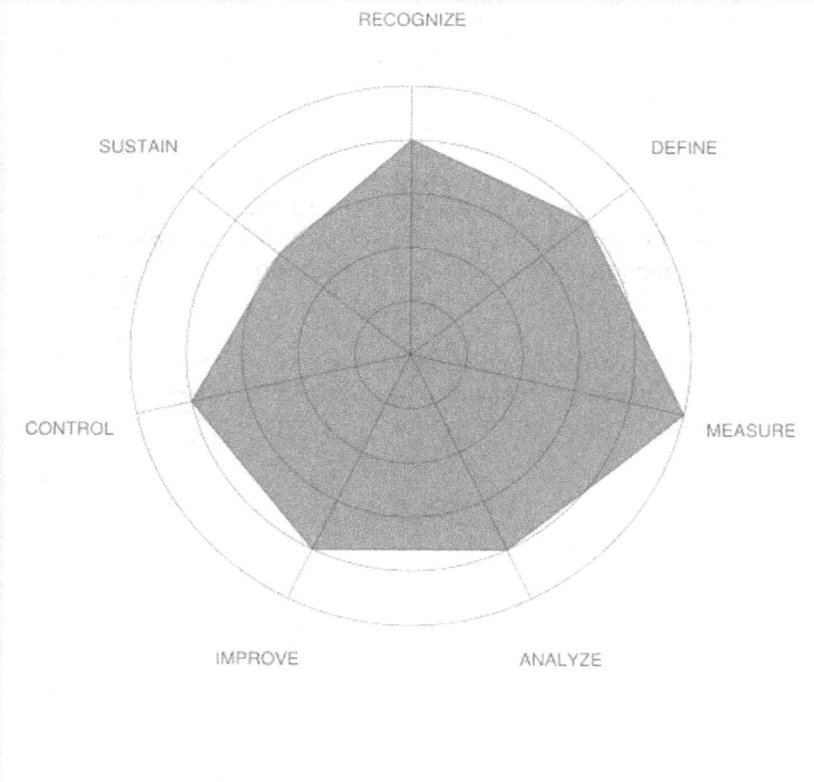

Managed UEM Scorecard

Your Scores:

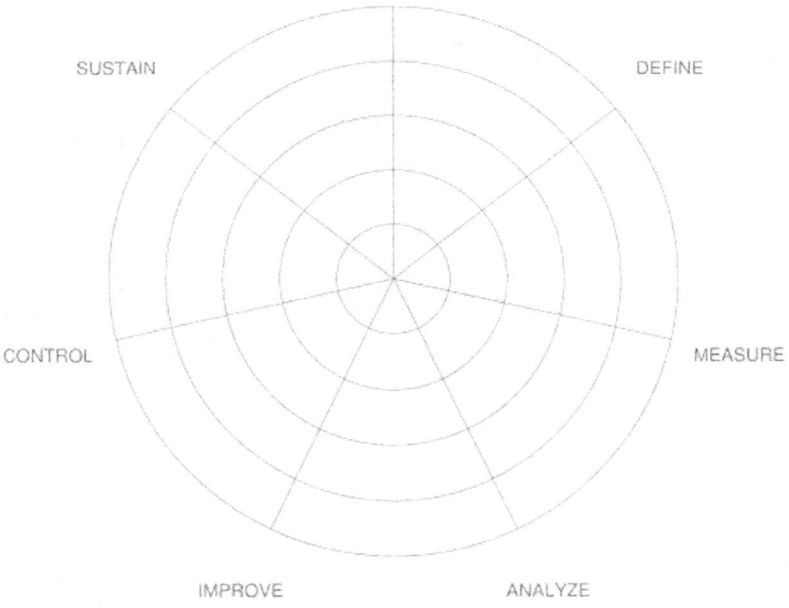

BEGINNING OF THE SELF-ASSESSMENT:

CRITERION #1: RECOGNIZE

INTENT: Be aware of the need for change. Recognize that there is an unfavorable variation, problem or symptom.

In my belief, the answer to this question is clearly defined:

5 Strongly Agree

4 Agree

3 Neutral

2 Disagree

1 Strongly Disagree

1. What are the Managed UEM resources needed?
<--- Score

2. What is the Managed UEM problem definition? What do you need to resolve?
<--- Score

3. What are your needs in relation to Managed UEM skills, labor, equipment, and markets?

<--- Score

4. Is it clear when you think of the day ahead of you what activities and tasks you need to complete?
<--- Score

5. Which issues are too important to ignore?
<--- Score

6. What prevents you from making the changes you know will make you a more effective Managed UEM leader?
<--- Score

7. Looking at each person individually – does every one have the qualities which are needed to work in this group?
<--- Score

8. What are the expected benefits of Managed UEM to the stakeholder?
<--- Score

9. What situation(s) led to this Managed UEM Self Assessment?
<--- Score

10. Who needs budgets?
<--- Score

11. What is the recognized need?
<--- Score

12. Do you know what you need to know about Managed UEM?
<--- Score

13. Do you have/need 24-hour access to key personnel?
<--- Score

14. Are problem definition and motivation clearly presented?
<--- Score

15. What would happen if Managed UEM weren't done?
<--- Score

16. How are the Managed UEM's objectives aligned to the group's overall stakeholder strategy?
<--- Score

17. What needs to be done?
<--- Score

18. What is the extent or complexity of the Managed UEM problem?
<--- Score

19. Will Managed UEM deliverables need to be tested and, if so, by whom?
<--- Score

20. What is the smallest subset of the problem you can usefully solve?
<--- Score

21. Are there Managed UEM problems defined?
<--- Score

22. How many trainings, in total, are needed?

<--- Score

23. Are employees recognized or rewarded for performance that demonstrates the highest levels of integrity?
<--- Score

24. Are controls defined to recognize and contain problems?
<--- Score

25. Who needs to know?
<--- Score

26. Have you identified your Managed UEM key performance indicators?
<--- Score

27. Will it solve real problems?
<--- Score

28. Whom do you really need or want to serve?
<--- Score

29. When a Managed UEM manager recognizes a problem, what options are available?
<--- Score

30. Who defines the rules in relation to any given issue?
<--- Score

31. Would you recognize a threat from the inside?
<--- Score

32. What extra resources will you need?

<--- Score

33. What Managed UEM capabilities do you need?
<--- Score

34. What do employees need in the short term?
<--- Score

35. As a sponsor, customer or management, how important is it to meet goals, objectives?
<--- Score

36. What resources or support might you need?
<--- Score

37. Is the quality assurance team identified?
<--- Score

38. Are there recognized Managed UEM problems?
<--- Score

39. Do you need to avoid or amend any Managed UEM activities?
<--- Score

40. For your Managed UEM project, identify and describe the business environment, is there more than one layer to the business environment?
<--- Score

41. What activities does the governance board need to consider?
<--- Score

42. What vendors make products that address the Managed UEM needs?

<--- Score

43. What information do users need?
<--- Score

44. To what extent would your organization benefit from being recognized as a award recipient?
<--- Score

45. Does your organization need more Managed UEM education?
<--- Score

46. How do you identify subcontractor relationships?
<--- Score

47. What does Managed UEM success mean to the stakeholders?
<--- Score

48. Consider your own Managed UEM project, what types of organizational problems do you think might be causing or affecting your problem, based on the work done so far?
<--- Score

49. Are there any specific expectations or concerns about the Managed UEM team, Managed UEM itself?
<--- Score

50. How are training requirements identified?
<--- Score

51. Are you dealing with any of the same issues today as yesterday? What can you do about this?

<--- Score

52. Does Managed UEM create potential expectations in other areas that need to be recognized and considered?
<--- Score

53. How do you recognize an objection?
<--- Score

54. Do you recognize Managed UEM achievements?
<--- Score

55. Do you need different information or graphics?
<--- Score

56. Who needs to know about Managed UEM?
<--- Score

57. What is the problem and/or vulnerability?
<--- Score

58. How do you take a forward-looking perspective in identifying Managed UEM research related to market response and models?
<--- Score

59. How can auditing be a preventative security measure?
<--- Score

60. Who needs what information?
<--- Score

61. What problems are you facing and how do you consider Managed UEM will circumvent those

obstacles?

<--- Score

62. Who should resolve the Managed UEM issues?

<--- Score

63. How much are sponsors, customers, partners, stakeholders involved in Managed UEM? In other words, what are the risks, if Managed UEM does not deliver successfully?

<--- Score

64. What training and capacity building actions are needed to implement proposed reforms?

<--- Score

65. Where is training needed?

<--- Score

66. What are the minority interests and what amount of minority interests can be recognized?

<--- Score

67. Which needs are not included or involved?

<--- Score

68. What are the timeframes required to resolve each of the issues/problems?

<--- Score

69. What are the stakeholder objectives to be achieved with Managed UEM?

<--- Score

70. Are there regulatory / compliance issues?

<--- Score

71. What should be considered when identifying available resources, constraints, and deadlines?
<--- Score

72. What Managed UEM coordination do you need?
<--- Score

73. Think about the people you identified for your Managed UEM project and the project responsibilities you would assign to them, what kind of training do you think they would need to perform these responsibilities effectively?
<--- Score

74. Why the need?
<--- Score

75. Is it needed?
<--- Score

76. Can management personnel recognize the monetary benefit of Managed UEM?
<--- Score

77. Are losses recognized in a timely manner?
<--- Score

78. How are you going to measure success?
<--- Score

79. What is the problem or issue?
<--- Score

80. To what extent does each concerned units

management team recognize Managed UEM as an effective investment?

<--- Score

81. How do you recognize an Managed UEM objection?

<--- Score

82. How do you assess your Managed UEM workforce capability and capacity needs, including skills, competencies, and staffing levels?

<--- Score

83. Are your goals realistic? Do you need to redefine your problem? Perhaps the problem has changed or maybe you have reached your goal and need to set a new one?

<--- Score

84. Where do you need to exercise leadership?

<--- Score

85. Will new equipment/products be required to facilitate Managed UEM delivery, for example is new software needed?

<--- Score

86. What Managed UEM events should you attend?

<--- Score

87. Will a response program recognize when a crisis occurs and provide some level of response?

<--- Score

88. Which information does the Managed UEM business case need to include?

<--- Score

89. What Managed UEM problem should be solved?
<--- Score

90. Who else hopes to benefit from it?
<--- Score

91. How do you identify the kinds of information that you will need?
<--- Score

92. Are there any revenue recognition issues?
<--- Score

93. What else needs to be measured?
<--- Score

94. Did you miss any major Managed UEM issues?
<--- Score

95. What are the clients issues and concerns?
<--- Score

Add up total points for this section:
_ _ _ _ _ = Total points for this section

Divided by: _ _ _ _ _ _ (number of
statements answered) = _ _ _ _ _ _
Average score for this section

Transfer your score to the Managed UEM
Index at the beginning of the Self-
Assessment.

CRITERION #2: DEFINE:

INTENT: Formulate the stakeholder problem. Define the problem, needs and objectives.

In my belief, the answer to this question is clearly defined:

5 Strongly Agree

4 Agree

3 Neutral

2 Disagree

1 Strongly Disagree

1. What gets examined?
<--- Score

2. How would you define the culture at your organization, how susceptible is it to Managed UEM changes?
<--- Score

3. How do you manage changes in Managed UEM

requirements?
<--- Score

4. Are resources adequate for the scope?
<--- Score

5. Do you have a Managed UEM success story or case study ready to tell and share?
<--- Score

6. Has anyone else (internal or external to the group) attempted to solve this problem or a similar one before? If so, what knowledge can be leveraged from these previous efforts?
<--- Score

7. Are roles and responsibilities formally defined?
<--- Score

8. What happens if Managed UEM's scope changes?
<--- Score

9. Have the customer needs been translated into specific, measurable requirements? How?
<--- Score

10. How often are the team meetings?
<--- Score

11. Has a project plan, Gantt chart, or similar been developed/completed?
<--- Score

12. What is the scope of the Managed UEM effort?
<--- Score

13. What system do you use for gathering Managed UEM information?
<--- Score

14. Who approved the Managed UEM scope?
<--- Score

15. How do you manage scope?
<--- Score

16. Why are you doing Managed UEM and what is the scope?
<--- Score

17. Is special Managed UEM user knowledge required?
<--- Score

18. What information should you gather?
<--- Score

19. How and when will the baselines be defined?
<--- Score

20. What are the Managed UEM tasks and definitions?
<--- Score

21. What critical content must be communicated – who, what, when, where, and how?
<--- Score

22. Is there a Managed UEM management charter, including stakeholder case, problem and goal statements, scope, milestones, roles and responsibilities, communication plan?
<--- Score

23. Are required metrics defined, what are they?
<--- Score

24. How do you catch Managed UEM definition inconsistencies?
<--- Score

25. What information do you gather?
<--- Score

26. What scope to assess?
<--- Score

27. How do you hand over Managed UEM context?
<--- Score

28. Is the team equipped with available and reliable resources?
<--- Score

29. Who is gathering information?
<--- Score

30. What sort of initial information to gather?
<--- Score

31. Are accountability and ownership for Managed UEM clearly defined?
<--- Score

32. What is in the scope and what is not in scope?
<--- Score

33. If substitutes have been appointed, have they been briefed on the Managed UEM goals and received

regular communications as to the progress to date?
<--- Score

34. How do you gather the stories?
<--- Score

35. The political context: who holds power?
<--- Score

36. What is the definition of Managed UEM excellence?
<--- Score

37. What are the core elements of the Managed UEM business case?
<--- Score

38. How do you build the right business case?
<--- Score

39. Is there any additional Managed UEM definition of success?
<--- Score

40. What intelligence can you gather?
<--- Score

41. Is Managed UEM linked to key stakeholder goals and objectives?
<--- Score

42. Have all basic functions of Managed UEM been defined?
<--- Score

43. Has the direction changed at all during the course

of Managed UEM? If so, when did it change and why?
<--- Score

44. Have all of the relationships been defined properly?
<--- Score

45. Are there any constraints known that bear on the ability to perform Managed UEM work? How is the team addressing them?
<--- Score

46. What is the scope of the Managed UEM work?
<--- Score

47. What is a worst-case scenario for losses?
<--- Score

48. Has the improvement team collected the 'voice of the customer' (obtained feedback – qualitative and quantitative)?
<--- Score

49. What defines best in class?
<--- Score

50. In what way can you redefine the criteria of choice clients have in your category in your favor?
<--- Score

51. What is the scope?
<--- Score

52. Has a Managed UEM requirement not been met?
<--- Score

53. Is there a completed, verified, and validated high-level 'as is' (not 'should be' or 'could be') stakeholder process map?
<--- Score

54. Will team members regularly document their Managed UEM work?
<--- Score

55. When is/was the Managed UEM start date?
<--- Score

56. Are the Managed UEM requirements complete?
<--- Score

57. What are the requirements for audit information?
<--- Score

58. What is in scope?
<--- Score

59. What are the compelling stakeholder reasons for embarking on Managed UEM?
<--- Score

60. Has a team charter been developed and communicated?
<--- Score

61. What baselines are required to be defined and managed?
<--- Score

62. Have specific policy objectives been defined?
<--- Score

63. Has the Managed UEM work been fairly and/ or equitably divided and delegated among team members who are qualified and capable to perform the work? Has everyone contributed?
<--- Score

64. Is the scope of Managed UEM defined?
<--- Score

65. What constraints exist that might impact the team?
<--- Score

66. Is Managed UEM currently on schedule according to the plan?
<--- Score

67. What is out-of-scope initially?
<--- Score

68. Will a Managed UEM production readiness review be required?
<--- Score

69. How was the 'as is' process map developed, reviewed, verified and validated?
<--- Score

70. Are the Managed UEM requirements testable?
<--- Score

71. Does the scope remain the same?
<--- Score

72. What are the rough order estimates on cost savings/opportunities that Managed UEM brings?

<--- Score

73. How are consistent Managed UEM definitions important?
<--- Score

74. How can the value of Managed UEM be defined?
<--- Score

75. Is there regularly 100% attendance at the team meetings? If not, have appointed substitutes attended to preserve cross-functionality and full representation?
<--- Score

76. Is the Managed UEM scope complete and appropriately sized?
<--- Score

77. Is data collected and displayed to better understand customer(s) critical needs and requirements.
<--- Score

78. What would be the goal or target for a Managed UEM's improvement team?
<--- Score

79. What is the scope of Managed UEM?
<--- Score

80. What are the Roles and Responsibilities for each team member and its leadership? Where is this documented?
<--- Score

81. Where can you gather more information?
<--- Score

82. What scope do you want your strategy to cover?
<--- Score

83. What Managed UEM services do you require?
<--- Score

84. Who is gathering Managed UEM information?
<--- Score

85. How do you gather requirements?
<--- Score

86. Are all requirements met?
<--- Score

87. Has everyone on the team, including the team leaders, been properly trained?
<--- Score

88. What is out of scope?
<--- Score

89. Is it clearly defined in and to your organization what you do?
<--- Score

90. How will the Managed UEM team and the group measure complete success of Managed UEM?
<--- Score

91. Are customer(s) identified and segmented according to their different needs and requirements?
<--- Score

92. How does the Managed UEM manager ensure against scope creep?
<--- Score

93. What was the context?
<--- Score

94. Are audit criteria, scope, frequency and methods defined?
<--- Score

95. Is the team adequately staffed with the desired cross-functionality? If not, what additional resources are available to the team?
<--- Score

96. Do you have organizational privacy requirements?
<--- Score

97. How is the team tracking and documenting its work?
<--- Score

98. What are the boundaries of the scope? What is in bounds and what is not? What is the start point? What is the stop point?
<--- Score

99. What Managed UEM requirements should be gathered?
<--- Score

100. What specifically is the problem? Where does it occur? When does it occur? What is its extent?
<--- Score

101. Are task requirements clearly defined?
<--- Score

102. Will team members perform Managed UEM work when assigned and in a timely fashion?
<--- Score

103. Has your scope been defined?
<--- Score

104. Is the improvement team aware of the different versions of a process: what they think it is vs. what it actually is vs. what it should be vs. what it could be?
<--- Score

105. Is there a completed SIPOC representation, describing the Suppliers, Inputs, Process, Outputs, and Customers?
<--- Score

106. Do you all define Managed UEM in the same way?
<--- Score

107. What are the Managed UEM use cases?
<--- Score

108. How do you manage unclear Managed UEM requirements?
<--- Score

109. What customer feedback methods were used to solicit their input?
<--- Score

110. Is the Managed UEM scope manageable?
<--- Score

111. How do you think the partners involved in Managed UEM would have defined success?
<--- Score

112. Who are the Managed UEM improvement team members, including Management Leads and Coaches?
<--- Score

113. What is the definition of success?
<--- Score

114. Is there a critical path to deliver Managed UEM results?
<--- Score

115. Has a high-level 'as is' process map been completed, verified and validated?
<--- Score

116. What are the dynamics of the communication plan?
<--- Score

117. Are approval levels defined for contracts and supplements to contracts?
<--- Score

118. Has/have the customer(s) been identified?
<--- Score

119. Are different versions of process maps needed to account for the different types of inputs?

<--- Score

120. What is the worst case scenario?
<--- Score

121. How do you gather Managed UEM requirements?
<--- Score

122. Do the problem and goal statements meet the SMART criteria (specific, measurable, attainable, relevant, and time-bound)?
<--- Score

123. When are meeting minutes sent out? Who is on the distribution list?
<--- Score

124. Who defines (or who defined) the rules and roles?
<--- Score

125. How did the Managed UEM manager receive input to the development of a Managed UEM improvement plan and the estimated completion dates/times of each activity?
<--- Score

126. How would you define Managed UEM leadership?
<--- Score

127. Are there different segments of customers?
<--- Score

128. What key stakeholder process output measure(s) does Managed UEM leverage and how?

<--- Score

129. Does the team have regular meetings?
<--- Score

130. How do you keep key subject matter experts in the loop?
<--- Score

131. What are the record-keeping requirements of Managed UEM activities?
<--- Score

132. Is the current 'as is' process being followed? If not, what are the discrepancies?
<--- Score

133. Is the work to date meeting requirements?
<--- Score

134. Is scope creep really all bad news?
<--- Score

135. Is Managed UEM required?
<--- Score

136. What are (control) requirements for Managed UEM Information?
<--- Score

137. What knowledge or experience is required?
<--- Score

138. How have you defined all Managed UEM requirements first?
<--- Score

139. When is the estimated completion date?
<--- Score

140. How will variation in the actual durations of each activity be dealt with to ensure that the expected Managed UEM results are met?
<--- Score

Add up total points for this section:
_____ = Total points for this section

Divided by: _____ (number of statements answered) = _____
Average score for this section

Transfer your score to the Managed UEM Index at the beginning of the Self-Assessment.

CRITERION #3: MEASURE:

INTENT: Gather the correct data.
Measure the current performance and
evolution of the situation.

In my belief, the answer to this
question is clearly defined:

5 Strongly Agree

4 Agree

3 Neutral

2 Disagree

1 Strongly Disagree

1. What could cause you to change course?
<--- Score

2. What does losing customers cost your organization?
<--- Score

3. What is the root cause(s) of the problem?
<--- Score

4. How sensitive must the Managed UEM strategy be to cost?
<--- Score

5. Did you tackle the cause or the symptom?
<--- Score

6. What methods are feasible and acceptable to estimate the impact of reforms?
<--- Score

7. What does your operating model cost?
<--- Score

8. What are the costs and benefits?
<--- Score

9. What does a Test Case verify?
<--- Score

10. Does a Managed UEM quantification method exist?
<--- Score

11. How can you reduce costs?
<--- Score

12. What causes extra work or rework?
<--- Score

13. Are Managed UEM vulnerabilities categorized and prioritized?
<--- Score

14. Are you taking your company in the direction of better and revenue or cheaper and cost?

<--- Score

15. What are hidden Managed UEM quality costs?
<--- Score

16. Who should receive measurement reports?
<--- Score

17. How do you measure efficient delivery of Managed UEM services?
<--- Score

18. What causes innovation to fail or succeed in your organization?
<--- Score

19. What do people want to verify?
<--- Score

20. What measurements are being captured?
<--- Score

21. Are there any easy-to-implement alternatives to Managed UEM? Sometimes other solutions are available that do not require the cost implications of a full-blown project?
<--- Score

22. Have you included everything in your Managed UEM cost models?
<--- Score

23. Does the Managed UEM task fit the client's priorities?
<--- Score

24. How will costs be allocated?
<--- Score

25. Why do the measurements/indicators matter?
<--- Score

26. Are missed Managed UEM opportunities costing your organization money?
<--- Score

27. Do you effectively measure and reward individual and team performance?
<--- Score

28. What are the types and number of measures to use?
<--- Score

29. How do you measure success?
<--- Score

30. How do you verify your resources?
<--- Score

31. What are the current costs of the Managed UEM process?
<--- Score

32. Are the Managed UEM benefits worth its costs?
<--- Score

33. How can you reduce the costs of obtaining inputs?
<--- Score

34. What drives O&M cost?

<--- Score

35. How frequently do you track Managed UEM measures?
<--- Score

36. How do you verify the authenticity of the data and information used?
<--- Score

37. When a disaster occurs, who gets priority?
<--- Score

38. What are your customers expectations and measures?
<--- Score

39. Have you made assumptions about the shape of the future, particularly its impact on your customers and competitors?
<--- Score

40. How do you verify the Managed UEM requirements quality?
<--- Score

41. How can you measure Managed UEM in a systematic way?
<--- Score

42. What can be used to verify compliance?
<--- Score

43. What are your operating costs?
<--- Score

44. Are actual costs in line with budgeted costs?
<--- Score

45. How will success or failure be measured?
<--- Score

46. Was a business case (cost/benefit) developed?
<--- Score

47. What happens if cost savings do not materialize?
<--- Score

48. How is the value delivered by Managed UEM being measured?
<--- Score

49. What are the Managed UEM investment costs?
<--- Score

50. What are the costs?
<--- Score

51. Are indirect costs charged to the Managed UEM program?
<--- Score

52. How do you prevent mis-estimating cost?
<--- Score

53. What are the costs of reform?
<--- Score

54. What causes investor action?
<--- Score

55. Are there competing Managed UEM priorities?
<--- Score

56. How do your measurements capture actionable Managed UEM information for use in exceeding your customers expectations and securing your customers engagement?
<--- Score

57. Has a cost center been established?
<--- Score

58. How will your organization measure success?
<--- Score

59. Is the cost worth the Managed UEM effort ?
<--- Score

60. What are allowable costs?
<--- Score

61. How is performance measured?
<--- Score

62. What are the Managed UEM key cost drivers?
<--- Score

63. How will you measure your Managed UEM effectiveness?
<--- Score

64. What disadvantage does this cause for the user?
<--- Score

65. What causes mismanagement?
<--- Score

66. How do you verify performance?
<--- Score

67. How long to keep data and how to manage retention costs?
<--- Score

68. Do you have a flow diagram of what happens?
<--- Score

69. What users will be impacted?
<--- Score

70. Are there measurements based on task performance?
<--- Score

71. What could cause delays in the schedule?
<--- Score

72. Which Managed UEM impacts are significant?
<--- Score

73. Who pays the cost?
<--- Score

74. How can you measure the performance?
<--- Score

75. How are costs allocated?
<--- Score

76. How are measurements made?
<--- Score

77. What are your key Managed UEM organizational performance measures, including key short and longer-term financial measures?
<--- Score

78. How do you verify if Managed UEM is built right?
<--- Score

79. What details are required of the Managed UEM cost structure?
<--- Score

80. What potential environmental factors impact the Managed UEM effort?
<--- Score

81. What harm might be caused?
<--- Score

82. What are the costs of delaying Managed UEM action?
<--- Score

83. What is measured? Why?
<--- Score

84. How to cause the change?
<--- Score

85. Is it possible to estimate the impact of unanticipated complexity such as wrong or failed assumptions, feedback, etcetera on proposed reforms?
<--- Score

86. What tests verify requirements?

<--- Score

87. At what cost?
<--- Score

88. How will you measure success?
<--- Score

89. Do you aggressively reward and promote the people who have the biggest impact on creating excellent Managed UEM services/products?
<--- Score

90. What evidence is there and what is measured?
<--- Score

91. What are the estimated costs of proposed changes?
<--- Score

92. What are your primary costs, revenues, assets?
<--- Score

93. Do you have any cost Managed UEM limitation requirements?
<--- Score

94. Is there an opportunity to verify requirements?
<--- Score

95. What is the total cost related to deploying Managed UEM, including any consulting or professional services?
<--- Score

96. Are you aware of what could cause a problem?

<--- Score

97. How do you measure lifecycle phases?
<--- Score

98. Where is it measured?
<--- Score

99. How can you manage cost down?
<--- Score

100. Are supply costs steady or fluctuating?
<--- Score

101. Is the solution cost-effective?
<--- Score

102. What do you measure and why?
<--- Score

103. Do the benefits outweigh the costs?
<--- Score

104. When are costs are incurred?
<--- Score

105. What relevant entities could be measured?
<--- Score

106. How will effects be measured?
<--- Score

107. What are the strategic priorities for this year?
<--- Score

108. What are the operational costs after Managed

UEM deployment?
<--- Score

109. Have design-to-cost goals been established?
<--- Score

110. How do you measure variability?
<--- Score

111. Does management have the right priorities among projects?
<--- Score

112. What is your decision requirements diagram?
<--- Score

113. How is progress measured?
<--- Score

114. Which costs should be taken into account?
<--- Score

115. What is your Managed UEM quality cost segregation study?
<--- Score

116. How do you aggregate measures across priorities?
<--- Score

117. What is the total fixed cost?
<--- Score

118. Are you able to realize any cost savings?
<--- Score

119. What measurements are possible, practicable and meaningful?
<--- Score

120. What is the cost of rework?
<--- Score

121. What are you verifying?
<--- Score

122. Will Managed UEM have an impact on current business continuity, disaster recovery processes and/or infrastructure?
<--- Score

123. Which measures and indicators matter?
<--- Score

124. How will measures be used to manage and adapt?
<--- Score

125. Do you have an issue in getting priority?
<--- Score

126. Among the Managed UEM product and service cost to be estimated, which is considered hardest to estimate?
<--- Score

127. How much does it cost?
<--- Score

128. How do you quantify and qualify impacts?
<--- Score

129. Why do you expend time and effort to implement measurement, for whom?
<--- Score

130. What are the uncertainties surrounding estimates of impact?
<--- Score

131. What would it cost to replace your technology?
<--- Score

132. How do you control the overall costs of your work processes?
<--- Score

133. Are the measurements objective?
<--- Score

Add up total points for this section:
_ _ _ _ _ = Total points for this section

Divided by: _ _ _ _ _ _ (number of statements answered) = _ _ _ _ _ _
Average score for this section

Transfer your score to the Managed UEM Index at the beginning of the Self-Assessment.

CRITERION #4: ANALYZE:

INTENT: Analyze causes, assumptions and hypotheses.

In my belief, the answer to this question is clearly defined:

5 Strongly Agree

4 Agree

3 Neutral

2 Disagree

1 Strongly Disagree

1. Do you understand your management processes today?
<--- Score

2. What successful thing are you doing today that may be blinding you to new growth opportunities?
<--- Score

3. What output to create?
<--- Score

4. Who gets your output?

<--- Score

5. What did the team gain from developing a sub-process map?

<--- Score

6. Have any additional benefits been identified that will result from closing all or most of the gaps?

<--- Score

7. What Managed UEM data do you gather or use now?

<--- Score

8. Should you invest in industry-recognized qualifications?

<--- Score

9. What types of data do your Managed UEM indicators require?

<--- Score

10. Were there any improvement opportunities identified from the process analysis?

<--- Score

11. What resources go in to get the desired output?

<--- Score

12. What data is gathered?

<--- Score

13. Do your employees have the opportunity to do what they do best everyday?

<--- Score

14. What is your organizations process which leads to recognition of value generation?
<--- Score

15. What are the Managed UEM design outputs?
<--- Score

16. Do staff qualifications match your project?
<--- Score

17. Where is Managed UEM data gathered?
<--- Score

18. Do you have the authority to produce the output?
<--- Score

19. Is there any way to speed up the process?
<--- Score

20. Where is the data coming from to measure compliance?
<--- Score

21. What other jobs or tasks affect the performance of the steps in the Managed UEM process?
<--- Score

22. What Managed UEM data should be collected?
<--- Score

23. What are the necessary qualifications?
<--- Score

24. Is the suppliers process defined and controlled?

<--- Score

25. What are the personnel training and qualifications required?
<--- Score

26. Were any designed experiments used to generate additional insight into the data analysis?
<--- Score

27. An organizationally feasible system request is one that considers the mission, goals and objectives of the organization, key questions are: is the Managed UEM solution request practical and will it solve a problem or take advantage of an opportunity to achieve company goals?
<--- Score

28. Was a detailed process map created to amplify critical steps of the 'as is' stakeholder process?
<--- Score

29. What process improvements will be needed?
<--- Score

30. How do you identify specific Managed UEM investment opportunities and emerging trends?
<--- Score

31. Is pre-qualification of suppliers carried out?
<--- Score

32. Did any additional data need to be collected?
<--- Score

33. How do you promote understanding that

opportunity for improvement is not criticism of the status quo, or the people who created the status quo?
<--- Score

34. How do you measure the operational performance of your key work systems and processes, including productivity, cycle time, and other appropriate measures of process effectiveness, efficiency, and innovation?
<--- Score

35. What data do you need to collect?
<--- Score

36. What controls do you have in place to protect data?
<--- Score

37. What methods do you use to gather Managed UEM data?
<--- Score

38. Who owns what data?
<--- Score

39. Did any value-added analysis or 'lean thinking' take place to identify some of the gaps shown on the 'as is' process map?
<--- Score

40. What qualifies as competition?
<--- Score

41. What does the data say about the performance of the stakeholder process?
<--- Score

42. What tools were used to generate the list of possible causes?
<--- Score

43. What internal processes need improvement?
<--- Score

44. What are your Managed UEM processes?
<--- Score

45. Identify an operational issue in your organization, for example, could a particular task be done more quickly or more efficiently by Managed UEM?
<--- Score

46. A compounding model resolution with available relevant data can often provide insight towards a solution methodology; which Managed UEM models, tools and techniques are necessary?
<--- Score

47. How do you implement and manage your work processes to ensure that they meet design requirements?
<--- Score

48. What will drive Managed UEM change?
<--- Score

49. Have you defined which data is gathered how?
<--- Score

50. Were Pareto charts (or similar) used to portray the 'heavy hitters' (or key sources of variation)?
<--- Score

51. Do several people in different organizational units assist with the Managed UEM process?
<--- Score

52. Is the final output clearly identified?
<--- Score

53. How do you use Managed UEM data and information to support organizational decision making and innovation?
<--- Score

54. How do you define collaboration and team output?
<--- Score

55. How will the Managed UEM data be captured?
<--- Score

56. How is the Managed UEM Value Stream Mapping managed?
<--- Score

57. How often will data be collected for measures?
<--- Score

58. How is Managed UEM data gathered?
<--- Score

59. How are outputs preserved and protected?
<--- Score

60. How will the change process be managed?
<--- Score

61. What qualifications are necessary?
<--- Score

62. What were the crucial 'moments of truth' on the process map?
<--- Score

63. Do you, as a leader, bounce back quickly from setbacks?
<--- Score

64. What is your organizations system for selecting qualified vendors?
<--- Score

65. Have the problem and goal statements been updated to reflect the additional knowledge gained from the analyze phase?
<--- Score

66. How difficult is it to qualify what Managed UEM ROI is?
<--- Score

67. How do you ensure that the Managed UEM opportunity is realistic?
<--- Score

68. What are the revised rough estimates of the financial savings/opportunity for Managed UEM improvements?
<--- Score

69. Is there an established change management process?
<--- Score

70. Are gaps between current performance and the goal performance identified?
<--- Score

71. What do you need to qualify?
<--- Score

72. Do your contracts/agreements contain data security obligations?
<--- Score

73. What training and qualifications will you need?
<--- Score

74. What are evaluation criteria for the output?
<--- Score

75. What systems/processes must you excel at?
<--- Score

76. How do your work systems and key work processes relate to and capitalize on your core competencies?
<--- Score

77. What are your key performance measures or indicators and in-process measures for the control and improvement of your Managed UEM processes?
<--- Score

78. Are your outputs consistent?
<--- Score

79. What are the best opportunities for value improvement?

<--- Score

80. What conclusions were drawn from the team's data collection and analysis? How did the team reach these conclusions?
<--- Score

81. What are your current levels and trends in key measures or indicators of Managed UEM product and process performance that are important to and directly serve your customers? How do these results compare with the performance of your competitors and other organizations with similar offerings?
<--- Score

82. Has data output been validated?
<--- Score

83. What tools were used to narrow the list of possible causes?
<--- Score

84. Are all staff in core Managed UEM subjects Highly Qualified?
<--- Score

85. How is data used for program management and improvement?
<--- Score

86. Is the gap/opportunity displayed and communicated in financial terms?
<--- Score

87. Is the performance gap determined?
<--- Score

88. Who will facilitate the team and process?
<--- Score

89. What is the oversight process?
<--- Score

90. Think about some of the processes you undertake within your organization, which do you own?
<--- Score

91. Are Managed UEM changes recognized early enough to be approved through the regular process?
<--- Score

92. How can risk management be tied procedurally to process elements?
<--- Score

93. What kind of crime could a potential new hire have committed that would not only not disqualify him/her from being hired by your organization, but would actually indicate that he/she might be a particularly good fit?
<--- Score

94. Who qualifies to gain access to data?
<--- Score

95. What other organizational variables, such as reward systems or communication systems, affect the performance of this Managed UEM process?
<--- Score

96. What qualifications do Managed UEM leaders need?

<--- Score

97. What are the Managed UEM business drivers?
<--- Score

98. What were the financial benefits resulting from any 'ground fruit or low-hanging fruit' (quick fixes)?
<--- Score

99. Can you add value to the current Managed UEM decision-making process (largely qualitative) by incorporating uncertainty modeling (more quantitative)?
<--- Score

100. What is the complexity of the output produced?
<--- Score

101. Record-keeping requirements flow from the records needed as inputs, outputs, controls and for transformation of a Managed UEM process, are the records needed as inputs to the Managed UEM process available?
<--- Score

102. Has an output goal been set?
<--- Score

103. How many input/output points does it require?
<--- Score

104. What quality tools were used to get through the analyze phase?
<--- Score

105. Was a cause-and-effect diagram used to explore the different types of causes (or sources of variation)?
<--- Score

106. How was the detailed process map generated, verified, and validated?
<--- Score

107. Is data and process analysis, root cause analysis and quantifying the gap/opportunity in place?
<--- Score

108. How has the Managed UEM data been gathered?
<--- Score

109. Are you missing Managed UEM opportunities?
<--- Score

110. What is the cost of poor quality as supported by the team's analysis?
<--- Score

111. Who will gather what data?
<--- Score

112. What are your outputs?
<--- Score

113. Which Managed UEM data should be retained?
<--- Score

114. Is the Managed UEM process severely broken such that a re-design is necessary?
<--- Score

115. How do mission and objectives affect the Managed UEM processes of your organization?
<--- Score

116. Who is involved in the management review process?
<--- Score

117. What, related to, Managed UEM processes does your organization outsource?
<--- Score

118. What information qualified as important?
<--- Score

119. What process should you select for improvement?
<--- Score

120. Think about the functions involved in your Managed UEM project, what processes flow from these functions?
<--- Score

121. What Managed UEM data should be managed?
<--- Score

122. What is the Value Stream Mapping?
<--- Score

123. What is the output?
<--- Score

124. Where can you get qualified talent today?
<--- Score

125. Who is involved with workflow mapping?
<--- Score

126. What are the disruptive Managed UEM technologies that enable your organization to radically change your business processes?
<--- Score

127. What are your best practices for minimizing Managed UEM project risk, while demonstrating incremental value and quick wins throughout the Managed UEM project lifecycle?
<--- Score

128. What Managed UEM metrics are outputs of the process?
<--- Score

129. Is there a strict change management process?
<--- Score

130. What qualifications are needed?
<--- Score

Add up total points for this section:
_ _ _ _ _ = Total points for this section

Divided by: _ _ _ _ _ _ (number of statements answered) = _ _ _ _ _ _
Average score for this section

Transfer your score to the Managed UEM Index at the beginning of the Self-Assessment.

CRITERION #5: IMPROVE:

INTENT: Develop a practical solution. Innovate, establish and test the solution and to measure the results.

In my belief, the answer to this question is clearly defined:

5 Strongly Agree

4 Agree

3 Neutral

2 Disagree

1 Strongly Disagree

1. Risk Identification: What are the possible risk events your organization faces in relation to Managed UEM?
<--- Score

2. How is continuous improvement applied to risk management?
<--- Score

3. How will you recognize and celebrate results?
<--- Score

4. How do you decide how much to remunerate an employee?
<--- Score

5. What actually has to improve and by how much?
<--- Score

6. If you could go back in time five years, what decision would you make differently? What is your best guess as to what decision you're making today you might regret five years from now?
<--- Score

7. Who are the Managed UEM decision makers?
<--- Score

8. What criteria will you use to assess your Managed UEM risks?
<--- Score

9. What tools were most useful during the improve phase?
<--- Score

10. What are your current levels and trends in key measures or indicators of workforce and leader development?
<--- Score

11. How will you know when its improved?
<--- Score

12. How can you improve performance?

<--- Score

13. Does the goal represent a desired result that can be measured?
<--- Score

14. Are the risks fully understood, reasonable and manageable?
<--- Score

15. Would you develop a Managed UEM Communication Strategy?
<--- Score

16. Are the most efficient solutions problem-specific?
<--- Score

17. How do you measure risk?
<--- Score

18. What are the concrete Managed UEM results?
<--- Score

19. Who manages supplier risk management in your organization?
<--- Score

20. Who are the key stakeholders for the Managed UEM evaluation?
<--- Score

21. What does the 'should be' process map/design look like?
<--- Score

22. Can you identify any significant risks or exposures

to Managed UEM third- parties (vendors, service providers, alliance partners etc) that concern you?
<--- Score

23. Risk events: what are the things that could go wrong?
<--- Score

24. How do you improve Managed UEM service perception, and satisfaction?
<--- Score

25. Do you need to do a usability evaluation?
<--- Score

26. How are Managed UEM risks managed?
<--- Score

27. What needs improvement? Why?
<--- Score

28. How do you improve your likelihood of success ?
<--- Score

29. What current systems have to be understood and/ or changed?
<--- Score

30. Who makes the Managed UEM decisions in your organization?
<--- Score

31. What tools were used to tap into the creativity and encourage 'outside the box' thinking?
<--- Score

32. Who will be responsible for making the decisions to include or exclude requested changes once Managed UEM is underway?
<--- Score

33. Are risk management tasks balanced centrally and locally?
<--- Score

34. How do you manage Managed UEM risk?
<--- Score

35. Who controls key decisions that will be made?
<--- Score

36. How scalable is your Managed UEM solution?
<--- Score

37. Where do you need Managed UEM improvement?
<--- Score

38. How do you go about comparing Managed UEM approaches/solutions?
<--- Score

39. How do you measure progress and evaluate training effectiveness?
<--- Score

40. What is the team's contingency plan for potential problems occurring in implementation?
<--- Score

41. What tools were used to evaluate the potential solutions?

<--- Score

42. What resources are required for the improvement efforts?
<--- Score

43. To what extent does management recognize Managed UEM as a tool to increase the results?
<--- Score

44. Are the key business and technology risks being managed?
<--- Score

45. Who controls the risk?
<--- Score

46. Are decisions made in a timely manner?
<--- Score

47. Who do you report Managed UEM results to?
<--- Score

48. What is Managed UEM's impact on utilizing the best solution(s)?
<--- Score

49. Are events managed to resolution?
<--- Score

50. Have you identified breakpoints and/or risk tolerances that will trigger broad consideration of a potential need for intervention or modification of strategy?
<--- Score

51. Who are the Managed UEM decision-makers?
<--- Score

52. Who will be using the results of the measurement activities?
<--- Score

53. Is there a high likelihood that any recommendations will achieve their intended results?
<--- Score

54. What risks do you need to manage?
<--- Score

55. Can the solution be designed and implemented within an acceptable time period?
<--- Score

56. Why improve in the first place?
<--- Score

57. Is the Managed UEM risk managed?
<--- Score

58. Is there any other Managed UEM solution?
<--- Score

59. What to do with the results or outcomes of measurements?
<--- Score

60. For estimation problems, how do you develop an estimation statement?
<--- Score

61. Is the Managed UEM documentation

thorough?
<--- Score

62. How do you deal with Managed UEM risk?
<--- Score

63. How are policy decisions made and where?
<--- Score

64. What is the risk?
<--- Score

65. What do you want to improve?
<--- Score

66. How will you know that a change is an improvement?
<--- Score

67. Have you achieved Managed UEM improvements?
<--- Score

68. How can you better manage risk?
<--- Score

69. How do you link measurement and risk?
<--- Score

70. What tools do you use once you have decided on a Managed UEM strategy and more importantly how do you choose?
<--- Score

71. What attendant changes will need to be made to ensure that the solution is successful?

<--- Score

72. How do you measure improved Managed UEM service perception, and satisfaction?
<--- Score

73. What were the underlying assumptions on the cost-benefit analysis?
<--- Score

74. How significant is the improvement in the eyes of the end user?
<--- Score

75. Managed UEM risk decisions: whose call Is It?
<--- Score

76. Where do the Managed UEM decisions reside?
<--- Score

77. How do you improve productivity?
<--- Score

78. Do you cover the five essential competencies: Communication, Collaboration,Innovation, Adaptability, and Leadership that improve an organizations ability to leverage the new Managed UEM in a volatile global economy?
<--- Score

79. Can you integrate quality management and risk management?
<--- Score

80. Do you combine technical expertise with business knowledge and Managed UEM Key topics include

lifecycles, development approaches, requirements and how to make a business case?
<--- Score

81. What error proofing will be done to address some of the discrepancies observed in the 'as is' process?
<--- Score

82. What is the Managed UEM's sustainability risk?
<--- Score

83. Do vendor agreements bring new compliance risk ?
<--- Score

84. What is the magnitude of the improvements?
<--- Score

85. Does a good decision guarantee a good outcome?
<--- Score

86. Are procedures documented for managing Managed UEM risks?
<--- Score

87. Is the scope clearly documented?
<--- Score

88. What are the expected Managed UEM results?
<--- Score

89. Is any Managed UEM documentation required?
<--- Score

90. What went well, what should change, what can improve?

<--- Score

91. Do those selected for the Managed UEM team have a good general understanding of what Managed UEM is all about?
<--- Score

92. What are the affordable Managed UEM risks?
<--- Score

93. Is the Managed UEM solution sustainable?
<--- Score

94. How do you mitigate Managed UEM risk?
<--- Score

95. Who manages Managed UEM risk?
<--- Score

96. Will the controls trigger any other risks?
<--- Score

97. Which Managed UEM solution is appropriate?
<--- Score

98. When you map the key players in your own work and the types/domains of relationships with them, which relationships do you find easy and which challenging, and why?
<--- Score

99. What can you do to improve?
<--- Score

100. Which of the recognised risks out of all risks can be most likely transferred?

<--- Score

101. How do the Managed UEM results compare with the performance of your competitors and other organizations with similar offerings?
<--- Score

102. Is the measure of success for Managed UEM understandable to a variety of people?
<--- Score

103. Who are the people involved in developing and implementing Managed UEM?
<--- Score

104. Is risk periodically assessed?
<--- Score

105. How does the team improve its work?
<--- Score

106. At what point will vulnerability assessments be performed once Managed UEM is put into production (e.g., ongoing Risk Management after implementation)?
<--- Score

107. In the past few months, what is the smallest change you have made that has had the biggest positive result? What was it about that small change that produced the large return?
<--- Score

108. What should a proof of concept or pilot accomplish?
<--- Score

109. Is Managed UEM documentation maintained?
<--- Score

110. Are risk triggers captured?
<--- Score

111. Is the solution technically practical?
<--- Score

112. How can the phases of Managed UEM development be identified?
<--- Score

113. How do you keep improving Managed UEM?
<--- Score

114. How can you improve Managed UEM?
<--- Score

115. Who should make the Managed UEM decisions?
<--- Score

116. How do you manage and improve your Managed UEM work systems to deliver customer value and achieve organizational success and sustainability?
<--- Score

117. What are the implications of the one critical Managed UEM decision 10 minutes, 10 months, and 10 years from now?
<--- Score

118. What improvements have been achieved?
<--- Score

119. What Managed UEM improvements can be made?
<--- Score

120. Who will be responsible for documenting the Managed UEM requirements in detail?
<--- Score

121. How risky is your organization?
<--- Score

122. What lessons, if any, from a pilot were incorporated into the design of the full-scale solution?
<--- Score

123. What area needs the greatest improvement?
<--- Score

124. What were the criteria for evaluating a Managed UEM pilot?
<--- Score

125. How will you measure the results?
<--- Score

126. Explorations of the frontiers of Managed UEM will help you build influence, improve Managed UEM, optimize decision making, and sustain change, what is your approach?
<--- Score

127. What is the implementation plan?
<--- Score

128. How can skill-level changes improve Managed UEM?

<--- Score

129. What are the Managed UEM security risks?
<--- Score

130. What communications are necessary to support the implementation of the solution?
<--- Score

131. How will you know that you have improved?
<--- Score

132. For decision problems, how do you develop a decision statement?
<--- Score

133. Is supporting Managed UEM documentation required?
<--- Score

Add up total points for this section:
_____ = Total points for this section

Divided by: _____ (number of statements answered) = _____
Average score for this section

Transfer your score to the Managed UEM Index at the beginning of the Self-Assessment.

CRITERION #6: CONTROL:

INTENT: Implement the practical solution. Maintain the performance and correct possible complications.

In my belief, the answer to this question is clearly defined:

5 Strongly Agree

4 Agree

3 Neutral

2 Disagree

1 Strongly Disagree

1. Who controls critical resources?
<--- Score

2. Against what alternative is success being measured?
<--- Score

3. How is change control managed?
<--- Score

4. Are operating procedures consistent?
<--- Score

5. What do your reports reflect?
<--- Score

6. How do senior leaders actions reflect a commitment to the organizations Managed UEM values?
<--- Score

7. Who has control over resources?
<--- Score

8. In the case of a Managed UEM project, the criteria for the audit derive from implementation objectives, an audit of a Managed UEM project involves assessing whether the recommendations outlined for implementation have been met, can you track that any Managed UEM project is implemented as planned, and is it working?
<--- Score

9. How do you select, collect, align, and integrate Managed UEM data and information for tracking daily operations and overall organizational performance, including progress relative to strategic objectives and action plans?
<--- Score

10. Is there a recommended audit plan for routine surveillance inspections of Managed UEM's gains?
<--- Score

11. How will the process owner and team be able to

hold the gains?
<--- Score

12. Has the improved process and its steps been standardized?
<--- Score

13. What adjustments to the strategies are needed?
<--- Score

14. Who is going to spread your message?
<--- Score

15. Does Managed UEM appropriately measure and monitor risk?
<--- Score

16. Is a response plan in place for when the input, process, or output measures indicate an 'out-of-control' condition?
<--- Score

17. What other areas of the group might benefit from the Managed UEM team's improvements, knowledge, and learning?
<--- Score

18. How can you best use all of your knowledge repositories to enhance learning and sharing?
<--- Score

19. How will new or emerging customer needs/ requirements be checked/communicated to orient the process toward meeting the new specifications and continually reducing variation?
<--- Score

20. Implementation Planning: is a pilot needed to test the changes before a full roll out occurs?
<--- Score

21. What should you measure to verify efficiency gains?
<--- Score

22. What do you measure to verify effectiveness gains?
<--- Score

23. Act/Adjust: What Do you Need to Do Differently?
<--- Score

24. How might the group capture best practices and lessons learned so as to leverage improvements?
<--- Score

25. What are the performance and scale of the Managed UEM tools?
<--- Score

26. Does the Managed UEM performance meet the customer's requirements?
<--- Score

27. Do the Managed UEM decisions you make today help people and the planet tomorrow?
<--- Score

28. Are documented procedures clear and easy to follow for the operators?
<--- Score

29. Is reporting being used or needed?
<--- Score

30. Are the planned controls working?
<--- Score

31. Are new process steps, standards, and documentation ingrained into normal operations?
<--- Score

32. How will report readings be checked to effectively monitor performance?
<--- Score

33. Where do ideas that reach policy makers and planners as proposals for Managed UEM strengthening and reform actually originate?
<--- Score

34. Is there a documented and implemented monitoring plan?
<--- Score

35. What is your theory of human motivation, and how does your compensation plan fit with that view?
<--- Score

36. Are there documented procedures?
<--- Score

37. What is the control/monitoring plan?
<--- Score

38. Will any special training be provided for results interpretation?
<--- Score

39. What is the best design framework for Managed UEM organization now that, in a post industrial-age if the top-down, command and control model is no longer relevant?

<--- Score

40. Does a troubleshooting guide exist or is it needed?

<--- Score

41. How do you spread information?

<--- Score

42. Is the Managed UEM test/monitoring cost justified?

<--- Score

43. How do you monitor usage and cost?

<--- Score

44. Have new or revised work instructions resulted?

<--- Score

45. Can support from partners be adjusted?

<--- Score

46. What should the next improvement project be that is related to Managed UEM?

<--- Score

47. How widespread is its use?

<--- Score

48. Are controls in place and consistently applied?

<--- Score

49. How will the day-to-day responsibilities for monitoring and continual improvement be transferred from the improvement team to the process owner?
<--- Score

50. Has the Managed UEM value of standards been quantified?
<--- Score

51. How will the process owner verify improvement in present and future sigma levels, process capabilities?
<--- Score

52. Can you adapt and adjust to changing Managed UEM situations?
<--- Score

53. Who sets the Managed UEM standards?
<--- Score

54. What other systems, operations, processes, and infrastructures (hiring practices, staffing, training, incentives/rewards, metrics/dashboards/scorecards, etc.) need updates, additions, changes, or deletions in order to facilitate knowledge transfer and improvements?
<--- Score

55. How do you encourage people to take control and responsibility?
<--- Score

56. Is a response plan established and deployed?
<--- Score

57. What Managed UEM standards are applicable?
<--- Score

58. What are your results for key measures or indicators of the accomplishment of your Managed UEM strategy and action plans, including building and strengthening core competencies?
<--- Score

59. Is there a transfer of ownership and knowledge to process owner and process team tasked with the responsibilities.
<--- Score

60. How do you plan for the cost of succession?
<--- Score

61. Are the planned controls in place?
<--- Score

62. Are you measuring, monitoring and predicting Managed UEM activities to optimize operations and profitability, and enhancing outcomes?
<--- Score

63. Do the viable solutions scale to future needs?
<--- Score

64. What are you attempting to measure/monitor?
<--- Score

65. Are pertinent alerts monitored, analyzed and distributed to appropriate personnel?
<--- Score

66. Do you monitor the effectiveness of your

Managed UEM activities?
<--- Score

67. What are the critical parameters to watch?
<--- Score

68. Do you monitor the Managed UEM decisions made and fine tune them as they evolve?
<--- Score

69. What is the standard for acceptable Managed UEM performance?
<--- Score

70. Is there a Managed UEM Communication plan covering who needs to get what information when?
<--- Score

71. Is new knowledge gained imbedded in the response plan?
<--- Score

72. What can you control?
<--- Score

73. Are the Managed UEM standards challenging?
<--- Score

74. Will the team be available to assist members in planning investigations?
<--- Score

75. How do you establish and deploy modified action plans if circumstances require a shift in plans and rapid execution of new plans?

<--- Score

76. Who is the Managed UEM process owner?
<--- Score

77. What are the known security controls?
<--- Score

78. Are suggested corrective/restorative actions indicated on the response plan for known causes to problems that might surface?
<--- Score

79. How is Managed UEM project cost planned, managed, monitored?
<--- Score

80. How do controls support value?
<--- Score

81. How do you plan on providing proper recognition and disclosure of supporting companies?
<--- Score

82. Does the response plan contain a definite closed loop continual improvement scheme (e.g., plan-do-check-act)?
<--- Score

83. What are the key elements of your Managed UEM performance improvement system, including your evaluation, organizational learning, and innovation processes?
<--- Score

84. What quality tools were useful in the control phase?
<--- Score

85. Is there an action plan in case of emergencies?
<--- Score

86. Is there a control plan in place for sustaining improvements (short and long-term)?
<--- Score

87. You may have created your quality measures at a time when you lacked resources, technology wasn't up to the required standard, or low service levels were the industry norm. Have those circumstances changed?
<--- Score

88. What is your plan to assess your security risks?
<--- Score

89. How likely is the current Managed UEM plan to come in on schedule or on budget?
<--- Score

90. Is knowledge gained on process shared and institutionalized?
<--- Score

91. Is there a standardized process?
<--- Score

92. What do you stand for--and what are you against?
<--- Score

93. How will you measure your QA plan's

effectiveness?
<--- Score

94. How will input, process, and output variables be checked to detect for sub-optimal conditions?
<--- Score

95. What is the recommended frequency of auditing?
<--- Score

96. How will Managed UEM decisions be made and monitored?
<--- Score

97. What key inputs and outputs are being measured on an ongoing basis?
<--- Score

98. What are customers monitoring?
<--- Score

99. Does job training on the documented procedures need to be part of the process team's education and training?
<--- Score

100. Who will be in control?
<--- Score

101. Is there documentation that will support the successful operation of the improvement?
<--- Score

Add up total points for this section:
_ _ _ _ _ = Total points for this section

Divided by: _____ (number of
statements answered) = _____
Average score for this section

Transfer your score to the Managed UEM
Index at the beginning of the Self-
Assessment.

CRITERION #7: SUSTAIN:

INTENT: Retain the benefits.

In my belief, the answer to this question is clearly defined:

5 Strongly Agree

4 Agree

3 Neutral

2 Disagree

1 Strongly Disagree

1. If no one would ever find out about your accomplishments, how would you lead differently?
<--- Score

2. What are your personal philosophies regarding Managed UEM and how do they influence your work?
<--- Score

3. Will it be accepted by users?
<--- Score

4. How do you keep the momentum going?
<--- Score

5. How can you become more high-tech but still be high touch?
<--- Score

6. What are the long-term Managed UEM goals?
<--- Score

7. What is your question? Why?
<--- Score

8. Is the Managed UEM organization completing tasks effectively and efficiently?
<--- Score

9. If you were responsible for initiating and implementing major changes in your organization, what steps might you take to ensure acceptance of those changes?
<--- Score

10. What will be the consequences to the stakeholder (financial, reputation etc) if Managed UEM does not go ahead or fails to deliver the objectives?
<--- Score

11. What would have to be true for the option on the table to be the best possible choice?
<--- Score

12. Operational - will it work?
<--- Score

13. What are the business goals Managed UEM is aiming to achieve?
<--- Score

14. Who is the main stakeholder, with ultimate responsibility for driving Managed UEM forward?
<--- Score

15. In a project to restructure Managed UEM outcomes, which stakeholders would you involve?
<--- Score

16. What is it like to work for you?
<--- Score

17. Are there any activities that you can take off your to do list?
<--- Score

18. Do Managed UEM rules make a reasonable demand on a users capabilities?
<--- Score

19. Which models, tools and techniques are necessary?
<--- Score

20. How are you doing compared to your industry?
<--- Score

21. How do you foster innovation?
<--- Score

22. How much does Managed UEM help?
<--- Score

23. What are strategies for increasing support and reducing opposition?
<--- Score

24. Who is responsible for errors?
<--- Score

25. Will there be any necessary staff changes (redundancies or new hires)?
<--- Score

26. What potential megatrends could make your business model obsolete?
<--- Score

27. In retrospect, of the projects that you pulled the plug on, what percent do you wish had been allowed to keep going, and what percent do you wish had ended earlier?
<--- Score

28. What is the craziest thing you can do?
<--- Score

29. At what moment would you think; Will I get fired?
<--- Score

30. Who, on the executive team or the board, has spoken to a customer recently?
<--- Score

31. Who are the key stakeholders?
<--- Score

32. If you do not follow, then how to lead?

<--- Score

33. What Managed UEM skills are most important?
<--- Score

34. What is the recommended frequency of auditing?
<--- Score

35. How do you lead with Managed UEM in mind?
<--- Score

36. If there were zero limitations, what would you do differently?
<--- Score

37. What happens if you do not have enough funding?
<--- Score

38. How important is Managed UEM to the user organizations mission?
<--- Score

39. Who have you, as a company, historically been when you've been at your best?
<--- Score

40. How do you manage Managed UEM Knowledge Management (KM)?
<--- Score

41. What would you recommend your friend do if he/she were facing this dilemma?
<--- Score

42. What you are going to do to affect the numbers?

<--- Score

43. Can the schedule be done in the given time?
<--- Score

44. What are your most important goals for the strategic Managed UEM objectives?
<--- Score

45. What are the barriers to increased Managed UEM production?
<--- Score

46. What are the potential basics of Managed UEM fraud?
<--- Score

47. Did your employees make progress today?
<--- Score

48. How do you govern and fulfill your societal responsibilities?
<--- Score

49. Who is responsible for Managed UEM?
<--- Score

50. How do you determine the key elements that affect Managed UEM workforce satisfaction, how are these elements determined for different workforce groups and segments?
<--- Score

51. How do you create buy-in?
<--- Score

52. Do you know what you are doing? And who do you call if you don't?
<--- Score

53. What knowledge, skills and characteristics mark a good Managed UEM project manager?
<--- Score

54. How can you negotiate Managed UEM successfully with a stubborn boss, an irate client, or a deceitful coworker?
<--- Score

55. Who will be responsible for deciding whether Managed UEM goes ahead or not after the initial investigations?
<--- Score

56. Do you have past Managed UEM successes?
<--- Score

57. What is the overall business strategy?
<--- Score

58. What are current Managed UEM paradigms?
<--- Score

59. How do senior leaders deploy your organizations vision and values through your leadership system, to the workforce, to key suppliers and partners, and to customers and other stakeholders, as appropriate?
<--- Score

60. What could happen if you do not do it?
<--- Score

61. How will you ensure you get what you expected?

<--- Score

62. How likely is it that a customer would recommend your company to a friend or colleague?

<--- Score

63. How do you maintain Managed UEM's Integrity?

<--- Score

64. Would you rather sell to knowledgeable and informed customers or to uninformed customers?

<--- Score

65. Do you think Managed UEM accomplishes the goals you expect it to accomplish?

<--- Score

66. What is the kind of project structure that would be appropriate for your Managed UEM project, should it be formal and complex, or can it be less formal and relatively simple?

<--- Score

67. If you got fired and a new hire took your place, what would she do different?

<--- Score

68. How do you proactively clarify deliverables and Managed UEM quality expectations?

<--- Score

69. Who are your customers?

<--- Score

70. What unique value proposition (UVP) do you offer?
<--- Score

71. Are the criteria for selecting recommendations stated?
<--- Score

72. What is the range of capabilities?
<--- Score

73. What have been your experiences in defining long range Managed UEM goals?
<--- Score

74. What is the estimated value of the project?
<--- Score

75. Is your basic point _____ or _____?
<--- Score

76. Who do you want your customers to become?
<--- Score

77. Why should people listen to you?
<--- Score

78. How do you know if you are successful?
<--- Score

79. In the past year, what have you done (or could you have done) to increase the accurate perception of your company/brand as ethical and honest?
<--- Score

80. Do you have enough freaky customers in your portfolio pushing you to the limit day in and day out?
<--- Score

81. What happens when a new employee joins the organization?
<--- Score

82. Which Managed UEM goals are the most important?
<--- Score

83. What trouble can you get into?
<--- Score

84. Who will manage the integration of tools?
<--- Score

85. What counts that you are not counting?
<--- Score

86. Who will provide the final approval of Managed UEM deliverables?
<--- Score

87. What is your BATNA (best alternative to a negotiated agreement)?
<--- Score

88. If you weren't already in this business, would you enter it today? And if not, what are you going to do about it?
<--- Score

89. How do you make it meaningful in connecting

Managed UEM with what users do day-to-day?
<--- Score

90. Who uses your product in ways you never expected?
<--- Score

91. Has implementation been effective in reaching specified objectives so far?
<--- Score

92. How will you know that the Managed UEM project has been successful?
<--- Score

93. Who are four people whose careers you have enhanced?
<--- Score

94. What role does communication play in the success or failure of a Managed UEM project?
<--- Score

95. What should you stop doing?
<--- Score

96. Why do and why don't your customers like your organization?
<--- Score

97. Do you have the right people on the bus?
<--- Score

98. Is your strategy driving your strategy? Or is the way in which you allocate resources driving your strategy?

<--- Score

99. What is the overall talent health of your organization as a whole at senior levels, and for each organization reporting to a member of the Senior Leadership Team?
<--- Score

100. How do you listen to customers to obtain actionable information?
<--- Score

101. To whom do you add value?
<--- Score

102. Are you paying enough attention to the partners your company depends on to succeed?
<--- Score

103. How much contingency will be available in the budget?
<--- Score

104. How do you stay inspired?
<--- Score

105. How do you assess the Managed UEM pitfalls that are inherent in implementing it?
<--- Score

106. How do you accomplish your long range Managed UEM goals?
<--- Score

107. What are you trying to prove to yourself, and how might it be hijacking your life and business success?

<--- Score

108. What are the success criteria that will indicate that Managed UEM objectives have been met and the benefits delivered?
<--- Score

109. Do you think you know, or do you know you know ?
<--- Score

110. How do you transition from the baseline to the target?
<--- Score

111. Can you maintain your growth without detracting from the factors that have contributed to your success?
<--- Score

112. How do you set Managed UEM stretch targets and how do you get people to not only participate in setting these stretch targets but also that they strive to achieve these?
<--- Score

113. Ask yourself: how would you do this work if you only had one staff member to do it?
<--- Score

114. How do customers see your organization?
<--- Score

115. Are you maintaining a past–present–future perspective throughout the Managed UEM discussion?

<--- Score

116. Is it economical; do you have the time and money?
<--- Score

117. What are the key enablers to make this Managed UEM move?
<--- Score

118. What may be the consequences for the performance of an organization if all stakeholders are not consulted regarding Managed UEM?
<--- Score

119. What one word do you want to own in the minds of your customers, employees, and partners?
<--- Score

120. Do you know who is a friend or a foe?
<--- Score

121. What are the challenges?
<--- Score

122. Why is it important to have senior management support for a Managed UEM project?
<--- Score

123. What stupid rule would you most like to kill?
<--- Score

124. Is there any reason to believe the opposite of my current belief?
<--- Score

125. Political -is anyone trying to undermine this project?
<--- Score

126. What is an unauthorized commitment?
<--- Score

127. Can you break it down?
<--- Score

128. Who do we want your customers to become?
<--- Score

129. Marketing budgets are tighter, consumers are more skeptical, and social media has changed forever the way we talk about Managed UEM, how do you gain traction?
<--- Score

130. What is the purpose of Managed UEM in relation to the mission?
<--- Score

131. Whose voice (department, ethnic group, women, older workers, etc) might you have missed hearing from in your company, and how might you amplify this voice to create positive momentum for your business?
<--- Score

132. Think of your Managed UEM project, what are the main functions?
<--- Score

133. Where can you break convention?

<--- Score

134. Are you using a design thinking approach and integrating Innovation, Managed UEM Experience, and Brand Value?
<--- Score

135. Who will determine interim and final deadlines?
<--- Score

136. Do you see more potential in people than they do in themselves?
<--- Score

137. Is a Managed UEM team work effort in place?
<--- Score

138. What are the short and long-term Managed UEM goals?
<--- Score

139. What trophy do you want on your mantle?
<--- Score

140. What management system can you use to leverage the Managed UEM experience, ideas, and concerns of the people closest to the work to be done?
<--- Score

141. How do you provide a safe environment -physically and emotionally?
<--- Score

142. What are the essentials of internal Managed UEM management?

<--- Score

143. Why should you adopt a Managed UEM framework?
<--- Score

144. If your customer were your grandmother, would you tell her to buy what you're selling?
<--- Score

145. What information is critical to your organization that your executives are ignoring?
<--- Score

146. If you had to leave your organization for a year and the only communication you could have with employees/colleagues was a single paragraph, what would you write?
<--- Score

147. How do you engage the workforce, in addition to satisfying them?
<--- Score

148. Are the assumptions believable and achievable?
<--- Score

149. How long will it take to change?
<--- Score

150. Are you / should you be revolutionary or evolutionary?
<--- Score

151. What is a feasible sequencing of reform initiatives over time?

<--- Score

152. Who is responsible for ensuring appropriate resources (time, people and money) are allocated to Managed UEM?
<--- Score

153. If you find that you havent accomplished one of the goals for one of the steps of the Managed UEM strategy, what will you do to fix it?
<--- Score

154. How can you incorporate support to ensure safe and effective use of Managed UEM into the services that you provide?
<--- Score

155. What goals did you miss?
<--- Score

156. What are the top 3 things at the forefront of your Managed UEM agendas for the next 3 years?
<--- Score

157. How is implementation research currently incorporated into each of your goals?
<--- Score

158. Is there any existing Managed UEM governance structure?
<--- Score

159. Do you feel that more should be done in the Managed UEM area?
<--- Score

160. Are assumptions made in Managed UEM stated explicitly?
<--- Score

161. What new services of functionality will be implemented next with Managed UEM ?
<--- Score

162. Are your responses positive or negative?
<--- Score

163. What have you done to protect your business from competitive encroachment?
<--- Score

164. If your company went out of business tomorrow, would anyone who doesn't get a paycheck here care?
<--- Score

165. What was the last experiment you ran?
<--- Score

166. How do you go about securing Managed UEM?
<--- Score

167. How will you motivate the stakeholders with the least vested interest?
<--- Score

168. What Managed UEM modifications can you make work for you?
<--- Score

169. Are you satisfied with your current role? If not, what is missing from it?
<--- Score

170. What are the gaps in your knowledge and experience?
<--- Score

171. Are you changing as fast as the world around you?
<--- Score

172. Are you making progress, and are you making progress as Managed UEM leaders?
<--- Score

173. How do you deal with Managed UEM changes?
<--- Score

174. What did you miss in the interview for the worst hire you ever made?
<--- Score

175. What is your Managed UEM strategy?
<--- Score

176. How can you become the company that would put you out of business?
<--- Score

177. Which individuals, teams or departments will be involved in Managed UEM?
<--- Score

178. How do you track customer value, profitability or financial return, organizational success, and sustainability?
<--- Score

179. What relationships among Managed UEM trends do you perceive?
<--- Score

180. Do you have an implicit bias for capital investments over people investments?
<--- Score

181. Do you say no to customers for no reason?
<--- Score

182. Who is on the team?
<--- Score

183. What is effective Managed UEM?
<--- Score

184. What must you excel at?
<--- Score

185. What does your signature ensure?
<--- Score

186. Who else should you help?
<--- Score

187. Which functions and people interact with the supplier and or customer?
<--- Score

188. Why is Managed UEM important for you now?
<--- Score

189. Can you do all this work?
<--- Score

190. When information truly is ubiquitous, when reach and connectivity are completely global, when computing resources are infinite, and when a whole new set of impossibilities are not only possible, but happening, what will that do to your business?

<--- Score

191. How will you insure seamless interoperability of Managed UEM moving forward?

<--- Score

192. Is Managed UEM realistic, or are you setting yourself up for failure?

<--- Score

193. What are the rules and assumptions your industry operates under? What if the opposite were true?

<--- Score

194. What projects are going on in the organization today, and what resources are those projects using from the resource pools?

<--- Score

195. What is the source of the strategies for Managed UEM strengthening and reform?

<--- Score

196. Are all key stakeholders present at all Structured Walkthroughs?

<--- Score

197. What is your competitive advantage?

<--- Score

198. What are the usability implications of Managed UEM actions?

<--- Score

199. If you had to rebuild your organization without any traditional competitive advantages (i.e., no killer technology, promising research, innovative product/ service delivery model, etcetera), how would your people have to approach their work and collaborate together in order to create the necessary conditions for success?

<--- Score

200. What are internal and external Managed UEM relations?

<--- Score

201. Who do you think the world wants your organization to be?

<--- Score

Add up total points for this section:

_ _ _ _ _ = Total points for this section

Divided by: _ _ _ _ _ _ (number of statements answered) = _ _ _ _ _ _ Average score for this section

Transfer your score to the Managed UEM Index at the beginning of the Self-Assessment.

Managed UEM and Managing Projects, Criteria for Project Managers:

1.0 Initiating Process Group: Managed UEM

1. What were things that you did very well and want to do the same again on the next Managed UEM project?

2. The Managed UEM project you are managing has nine stakeholders. How many channel of communications are there between corresponding stakeholders?

3. Which six sigma dmaic phase focuses on why and how defects and errors occur?

4. Are the changes in your Managed UEM project being formally requested, analyzed, and approved by the appropriate decision makers?

5. Who is involved in each phase?

6. Does the Managed UEM project team have enough people to execute the Managed UEM project plan?

7. Specific - is the objective clear in terms of what, how, when, and where the situation will be changed?

8. At which cmmi level are software processes documented, standardized, and integrated into a standard to-be practiced process for your organization?

9. Who are the Managed UEM project stakeholders?

10. Were resources available as planned?

11. Did you use a contractor or vendor?

12. Who is performing the work of the Managed UEM project?

13. Contingency planning. if a risk event occurs, what will you do?

14. At which stage, in a typical Managed UEM project do stake holders have maximum influence?

15. Based on your Managed UEM project communication management plan, what worked well?

16. Professionals want to know what is expected from them what are the deliverables?

17. Were decisions made in a timely manner?

18. What is the stake of others in your Managed UEM project?

19. What were things that you need to improve?

20. How can you make your needs known?

1.1 Project Charter: Managed UEM

21. What metrics could you look at?

22. How high should you set your goals?

23. Who manages integration?

24. What are you trying to accomplish?

25. Managed UEM project deliverables: what is the Managed UEM project going to produce?

26. For whom?

27. What is the purpose of the Managed UEM project?

28. Pop quiz – which are the same inputs as in the Managed UEM project charter?

29. Are you building in-house ?

30. How are Managed UEM projects different from operations?

31. Why have you chosen the aim you have set forth?

32. When do you use a Managed UEM project Charter?

33. Who are the stakeholders?

34. Assumptions: what factors, for planning purposes, are you considering to be true?

35. Will this replace an existing product?

36. Run it as as a startup?

37. Why do you need to manage scope?

38. What changes can you make to improve?

39. What are the constraints?

1.2 Stakeholder Register: Managed UEM

40. What opportunities exist to provide communications?

41. How big is the gap?

42. How will reports be created?

43. What & Why?

44. How much influence do they have on the Managed UEM project?

45. Is your organization ready for change?

46. What are the major Managed UEM project milestones requiring communications or providing communications opportunities?

47. Who is managing stakeholder engagement?

48. What is the power of the stakeholder?

49. Who wants to talk about Security?

50. How should employers make voices heard?

1.3 Stakeholder Analysis Matrix: Managed UEM

51. What do you need to appraise?

52. Competitive advantages?

53. Who can contribute financial or technical resources towards the work?

54. What is the range you need to look at?

55. How to measure the achievement of the Development Objective?

56. Cultural, attitudinal, behavioural?

57. What is the stakeholders name, what is function?

58. Who is influential in the Managed UEM project area (both thematic and geographic areas)?

59. Who determines value?

60. Guiding question: what is the issue at stake?

61. How do you manage Managed UEM project Risk?

62. Management cover, succession?

63. Are there different rules or organizational models for men and women?

64. Legislative effects?

65. Who are potential allies and opponents?

66. New markets, vertical, horizontal?

67. Vulnerable groups; who are the vulnerable groups that might be affected by the Managed UEM project?

68. Financial reserves, likely returns?

69. How to involve media?

70. What do you Evaluate?

2.0 Planning Process Group: Managed UEM

71. What type of estimation method are you using?

72. How well defined and documented are the Managed UEM project management processes you chose to use?

73. What is the difference between the early schedule and late schedule?

74. What factors are contributing to progress or delay in the achievement of products and results?

75. To what extent are the participating departments coordinating with each other?

76. What is the NEXT thing to do?

77. If a risk event occurs, what will you do?

78. When will the Managed UEM project be done?

79. Will you be replaced?

80. Product breakdown structure (pbs): what is the Managed UEM project result or product, and how should it look like, what are its parts?

81. What do they need to know about the Managed UEM project?

82. Is the Managed UEM project supported by national and/or local organizations?

83. Are the necessary foundations in place to ensure the sustainability of the results of the Managed UEM project?

84. To what extent have the target population and participants made the activities own, taking an active role in it?

85. Is the pace of implementing the products of the program ensuring the completeness of the results of the Managed UEM project?

86. Is your organization showing technical capacity and leadership commitment to keep working with the Managed UEM project and to repeat it?

87. To what extent has the intervention strategy been adapted to the areas of intervention in which it is being implemented?

88. How well do the team follow the chosen processes?

89. How many days can task X be late in starting without affecting the Managed UEM project completion date?

90. What will you do?

2.1 Project Management Plan: Managed UEM

91. Is there an incremental analysis/cost effectiveness analysis of proposed mitigation features based on an approved method and using an accepted model?

92. What data/reports/tools/etc. do program managers need?

93. Are there any windfall benefits that would accrue to the Managed UEM project sponsor or other parties?

94. What is the business need?

95. Are there any client staffing expectations?

96. What happened during the process that you found interesting?

97. Why Change?

98. What would you do differently?

99. How do you manage time?

100. Is the budget realistic?

101. Will you add a schedule and diagram?

102. What are the known stakeholder requirements?

103. What did not work so well?

104. Does the implementation plan have an appropriate division of responsibilities?

105. Do the proposed changes from the Managed UEM project include any significant risks to safety?

106. How well are you able to manage your risk?

107. Is the appropriate plan selected based on your organizations objectives and evaluation criteria expressed in Principles and Guidelines policies?

108. Are there non-structural buyout or relocation recommendations?

109. When is the Managed UEM project management plan created?

2.2 Scope Management Plan: Managed UEM

110. Deliverables -are the deliverables tangible and verifiable?

111. Are there checklists created to demine if all quality processes are followed?

112. What is the relative power of the Managed UEM project manager?

113. Function of the configuration control board?

114. What strengths do you have?

115. Are vendor invoices audited for accuracy before payment?

116. Assess the expected stability of the scope of this Managed UEM project how likely is it to change, how frequently, and by how much?

117. Pop quiz – what changed on Managed UEM project scope statement input?

118. Does the quality assurance process provide objective verification of adherence to applicable standards, procedures & requirements?

119. Has the Managed UEM project approach and development strategy of the Managed UEM project been defined, documented and accepted by the

appropriate stakeholders?

120. What are the risks that could significantly affect the communication on the Managed UEM project?

121. Have stakeholder accountabilities & responsibilities been clearly defined?

122. Are the results of quality assurance reviews provided to affected groups & individuals?

123. Have all necessary approvals been obtained?

124. Are the schedule estimates reasonable given the Managed UEM project?

125. Are you meeting with stake holders and team members?

126. Are all key components of a Quality Assurance Plan present?

127. Have adequate procedures been put in place for Managed UEM project communication and status reporting across Managed UEM project boundaries (for example interdependent software development among interfacing systems)?

128. Will your organizations estimating methodology be used and followed?

129. Does the Managed UEM project team have the skills necessary to successfully complete current Managed UEM project(s) and support the application?

2.3 Requirements Management Plan: Managed UEM

130. Is it new or replacing an existing business system or process?

131. Is any organizational data being used or stored?

132. How will requirements be managed?

133. Are actual resources expenditures versus planned expenditures acceptable?

134. What cost metrics will be used?

135. Is there formal agreement on who has authority to request a change in requirements?

136. How will the requirements become prioritized?

137. Which hardware or software, related to, or as outcome of the Managed UEM project is new to your organization?

138. Controlling Managed UEM project requirements involves monitoring the status of the Managed UEM project requirements and managing changes to the requirements. Who is responsible for monitoring and tracking the Managed UEM project requirements?

139. Do you have price sheets and a methodology for determining the total proposal cost?

140. How do you know that you have done this right?

141. Will you perform a Requirements Risk assessment and develop a plan to deal with risks?

142. When and how will a requirements baseline be established in this Managed UEM project?

143. In case of software development; Should you have a test for each code module?

144. Is the system software (non-operating system) new to the IT Managed UEM project team?

145. Has the requirements team been instructed in the Change Control process?

146. Did you use declarative statements?

147. Are all the stakeholders ready for the transition into the user community?

148. Do you have an agreed upon process for alerting the Managed UEM project Manager if a request for change in requirements leads to a product scope change?

149. How will you develop the schedule of requirements activities?

2.4 Requirements Documentation: Managed UEM

150. Basic work/business process; high-level, what is being touched?

151. How do you get the user to tell you what they want?

152. How to document system requirements?

153. How does what is being described meet the business need?

154. Where are business rules being captured?

155. What happens when requirements are wrong?

156. Is new technology needed?

157. Can the requirements be checked?

158. How can you document system requirements?

159. What are the attributes of a customer?

160. What will be the integration problems?

161. Where do you define what is a customer, what are the attributes of customer?

162. Who is interacting with the system?

163. How linear / iterative is your Requirements Gathering process (or will it be)?

164. Verifiability. can the requirements be checked?

165. What is the risk associated with cost and schedule?

166. What is effective documentation?

167. If applicable; are there issues linked with the fact that this is an offshore Managed UEM project?

168. What images does it conjure?

169. What can tools do for us?

2.5 Requirements Traceability Matrix: Managed UEM

170. Do you have a clear understanding of all subcontracts in place?

171. Will you use a Requirements Traceability Matrix?

172. How will it affect the stakeholders personally in career?

173. Why do you manage scope?

174. How do you manage scope?

175. Is there a requirements traceability process in place?

176. What is the WBS?

177. Describe the process for approving requirements so they can be added to the traceability matrix and Managed UEM project work can be performed. Will the Managed UEM project requirements become approved in writing?

178. What are the chronologies, contingencies, consequences, criteria?

179. What percentage of Managed UEM projects are producing traceability matrices between requirements and other work products?

180. Why use a WBS?

181. How small is small enough?

2.6 Project Scope Statement: Managed UEM

182. What should you drop in order to add something new?

183. Relevant - ask yourself can you get there; why are you doing this Managed UEM project?

184. Who will you recommend approve the change, and when do you recommend the change reviews occur?

185. Is your organization structure appropriate for the Managed UEM projects size and complexity?

186. Is there a Change Management Board?

187. Was planning completed before the Managed UEM project was initiated?

188. Will the risk documents be filed?

189. Do you anticipate new stakeholders joining the Managed UEM project over time?

190. Will the risk status be reported to management on a regular and frequent basis?

191. Once its defined, what is the stability of the Managed UEM project scope?

192. Are there issues that could affect the existing

requirements for the result, service, or product if the scope changes?

193. Were potential customers involved early in the planning process?

194. Is the quality function identified and assigned?

195. Has the format for tracking and monitoring schedules and costs been defined?

196. What is the product of this Managed UEM project?

197. Is this process communicated to the customer and team members?

198. Have you been able to easily identify success criteria and create objective measurements for each of the Managed UEM project scopes goal statements?

199. What is the most common tool for helping define the detail?

200. Will there be a Change Control Process in place?

201. Have the reports to be produced, distributed, and filed been defined?

2.7 Assumption and Constraint Log: Managed UEM

202. Contradictory information between document sections?

203. Are there standards for code development?

204. Is there a Steering Committee in place?

205. Are processes for release management of new development from coding and unit testing, to integration testing, to training, and production defined and followed?

206. Would known impacts serve as impediments?

207. Does the traceability documentation describe the tool and/or mechanism to be used to capture traceability throughout the life cycle?

208. Have adequate resources been provided by management to ensure Managed UEM project success?

209. Have Managed UEM project management standards and procedures been established and documented?

210. Is staff trained on the software technologies that are being used on the Managed UEM project?

211. Was the document/deliverable developed per

the appropriate or required standards (for example, Institute of Electrical and Electronics Engineers standards)?

212. Have all stakeholders been identified?

213. Are formal code reviews conducted?

214. Can the requirements be traced to the appropriate components of the solution, as well as test scripts?

215. What weaknesses do you have?

216. Is the process working, and people are not executing in compliance of the process?

217. Does the plan conform to standards?

218. Are requirements management tracking tools and procedures in place?

219. Do you know what your customers expectations are regarding this process?

220. What threats might prevent you from getting there?

221. What do you audit?

2.8 Work Breakdown Structure: Managed UEM

222. What is the probability of completing the Managed UEM project in less that xx days?

223. Is it still viable?

224. Is the work breakdown structure (wbs) defined and is the scope of the Managed UEM project clear with assigned deliverable owners?

225. What is the probability that the Managed UEM project duration will exceed xx weeks?

226. What has to be done?

227. When does it have to be done?

228. How big is a work-package?

229. Why would you develop a Work Breakdown Structure?

230. How many levels?

231. Can you make it?

232. When do you stop?

233. How will you and your Managed UEM project team define the Managed UEM projects scope and work breakdown structure?

234. Who has to do it?

235. Why is it useful?

236. Where does it take place?

237. How much detail?

2.9 WBS Dictionary: Managed UEM

238. Are the rates for allocating costs from each indirect cost pool to contracts updated as necessary to ensure a realistic monthly allocation of indirect costs without significant year-end adjustments?

239. Are internal budgets for authorized, and not priced changes based on the contractors resource plan for accomplishing the work?

240. Is undistributed budget limited to contract effort which cannot yet be planned to CWBS elements at or below the level specified for reporting to the Government?

241. Are budgets or values assigned to work packages and planning packages in terms of dollars, hours, or other measurable units?

242. The Managed UEM projected business base for each period?

243. The already stated responsible for overhead performance control of related costs?

244. Does the contractors system description or procedures require that the performance measurement baseline plus management reserve equal the contract budget base?

245. Are overhead costs budgets established on a basis consistent with anticipated direct business base?

246. Do the lines of authority for incurring indirect costs correspond to the lines of responsibility for management control of the same components of costs?

247. Is the work done on a work package level as described in the WBS dictionary?

248. Is cost performance measurement at the point in time most suitable for the category of material involved, and no earlier than the time of actual receipt of material?

249. Changes in the current direct and Managed UEM projected base?

250. Are the bases and rates for allocating costs from each indirect pool to commercial work consistent with the already stated used to allocate corresponding costs to Government contracts?

251. Contractor financial periods; for example, annual?

252. What is the goal?

253. Are the requirements for all items of overhead established by rational, traceable processes?

254. Detailed schedules which support control account and work package start and completion dates/events?

255. Does the contractors system provide for the determination of cost variances attributable to the

excess usage of material?

256. Is subcontracted work defined and identified to the appropriate subcontractor within the proper WBS element?

2.10 Schedule Management Plan: Managed UEM

257. Has the business need been clearly defined?

258. Has a resource management plan been created?

259. Where is the scheduling tool and who has access to it to view it?

260. Is there a formal process for updating the Managed UEM project baseline?

261. Which status reports are received per the Managed UEM project Plan?

262. Will the tools selected accomplish the scheduling needs?

263. Is there a procedure for management, control and release of schedule margin?

264. Are vendor contract reports, reviews and visits conducted periodically?

265. Has your organization readiness assessment been conducted?

266. Does the Managed UEM project have a Statement of Work?

267. Are Managed UEM project team members committed fulltime?

268. Has the Managed UEM project scope been baselined?

269. Is a process defined to measure the performance of the schedule management process itself?

270. Have all involved Managed UEM project stakeholders and work groups committed to the Managed UEM project?

271. Are meeting minutes captured and sent out after the meeting?

272. Are the schedule estimates reasonable given the Managed UEM project?

273. Have Managed UEM project success criteria been defined?

274. Who is responsible for estimating the activity durations?

275. Does the Managed UEM project have quality set of schedule BOEs?

276. Have key stakeholders been identified?

2.11 Activity List: Managed UEM

277. How detailed should a Managed UEM project get?

278. What went well?

279. The wbs is developed as part of a joint planning session. and how do you know that youhave done this right?

280. How much slack is available in the Managed UEM project?

281. When will the work be performed?

282. Is infrastructure setup part of your Managed UEM project?

283. Where will it be performed?

284. What went right?

285. How should ongoing costs be monitored to try to keep the Managed UEM project within budget?

286. Should you include sub-activities?

287. Who will perform the work?

288. How do you determine the late start (LS) for each activity?

289. How will it be performed?

290. What is your organizations history in doing similar activities?

291. For other activities, how much delay can be tolerated?

292. What will be performed?

293. What are you counting on?

294. Are the required resources available or need to be acquired?

295. What is the probability the Managed UEM project can be completed in xx weeks?

296. When do the individual activities need to start and finish?

2.12 Activity Attributes: Managed UEM

297. How much activity detail is required?

298. What activity do you think you should spend the most time on?

299. Activity: fair or not fair?

300. How difficult will it be to do specific activities on this Managed UEM project?

301. Resources to accomplish the work?

302. Have constraints been applied to the start and finish milestones for the phases?

303. Time for overtime?

304. How many days do you need to complete the work scope with a limit of X number of resources?

305. How difficult will it be to complete specific activities on this Managed UEM project?

306. Can you re-assign any activities to another resource to resolve an over-allocation?

307. Does your organization of the data change its meaning?

308. What is missing?

309. Have you identified the Activity Leveling Priority code value on each activity?

310. Has management defined a definite timeframe for the turnaround or Managed UEM project window?

311. Can more resources be added?

312. Do you feel very comfortable with your prediction?

313. How many resources do you need to complete the work scope within a limit of X number of days?

2.13 Milestone List: Managed UEM

314. What would happen if a delivery of material was one week late?

315. Insurmountable weaknesses?

316. What date will the task finish?

317. Can you derive how soon can the whole Managed UEM project finish?

318. What is the market for your technology, product or service?

319. Do you foresee any technical risks or developmental challenges?

320. Political effects?

321. When will the Managed UEM project be complete?

322. How late can the activity finish?

323. Gaps in capabilities?

324. How late can each activity be finished and started?

325. Describe the concept of the technology, product or service that will be or has been developed. How will it be used?

326. Global influences?

327. What are your competitors vulnerabilities?

328. Describe your organizations strengths and core competencies. What factors will make your organization succeed?

329. What background experience, skills, and strengths does the team bring to your organization?

330. Continuity, supply chain robustness?

331. Effects on core activities, distraction?

332. Identify critical paths (one or more) and which activities are on the critical path?

333. Environmental effects?

2.14 Network Diagram: Managed UEM

334. What are the Key Success Factors?

335. What must be completed before an activity can be started?

336. What is the probability of completing the Managed UEM project in less that xx days?

337. What is the lowest cost to complete this Managed UEM project in xx weeks?

338. Exercise: what is the probability that the Managed UEM project duration will exceed xx weeks?

339. Are the gantt chart and/or network diagram updated periodically and used to assess the overall Managed UEM project timetable?

340. What to do and When?

341. Will crashing x weeks return more in benefits than it costs?

342. What controls the start and finish of a job?

343. How confident can you be in your milestone dates and the delivery date?

344. What are the Major Administrative Issues?

345. What activities must follow this activity?

346. What job or jobs follow it?

347. If a current contract exists, can you provide the vendor name, contract start, and contract expiration date?

348. Review the logical flow of the network diagram. Take a look at which activities you have first and then sequence the activities. Do they make sense?

349. What is the completion time?

350. Are you on time?

351. Which type of network diagram allows you to depict four types of dependencies?

352. What are the tools?

353. What job or jobs could run concurrently?

2.15 Activity Resource Requirements: Managed UEM

354. Anything else?

355. How many signatures do you require on a check and does this match what is in your policy and procedures?

356. Is there anything planned that does not need to be here?

357. Are there unresolved issues that need to be addressed?

358. How do you handle petty cash?

359. What is the Work Plan Standard?

360. Which logical relationship does the PDM use most often?

361. When does monitoring begin?

362. What are constraints that you might find during the Human Resource Planning process?

363. Do you use tools like decomposition and rolling-wave planning to produce the activity list and other outputs?

364. Other support in specific areas?

365. Organizational Applicability?

366. Why do you do that?

2.16 Resource Breakdown Structure: Managed UEM

367. How can this help you with team building?

368. Who will be used as a Managed UEM project team member?

369. Which resources should be in the resource pool?

370. What defines a successful Managed UEM project?

371. Who will use the system?

372. Why is this important?

373. Changes based on input from stakeholders?

374. How should the information be delivered?

375. What is each stakeholders desired outcome for the Managed UEM project?

376. What is the difference between % Complete and % work?

377. Who delivers the information?

378. What is the purpose of assigning and documenting responsibility?

379. What is Managed UEM project communication management?

380. What can you do to improve productivity?

381. Which resource planning tool provides information on resource responsibility and accountability?

382. Are the required resources available?

383. What went wrong?

384. How difficult will it be to do specific activities on this Managed UEM project?

385. What defines a successful Managed UEM project?

2.17 Activity Duration Estimates: Managed UEM

386. Are team building activities completed to improve team performance?

387. Are procedures followed to ensure information is available to stakeholders in a timely manner?

388. Consider the history of modern quality management. How have experts such as Deming, Juran, Crosby, and Taguchi affected the quality movement and todays use of Six Sigma?

389. How can others help Managed UEM project managers understand your organizational context for Managed UEM projects?

390. Do you think many information technology professionals have experience writing RFPs and evaluating proposals for information technology Managed UEM projects?

391. How have experts such as Deming, Juran, Crosby, and Taguchi affected the quality movement and todays use of Six Sigma?

392. What is the duration of a milestone?

393. What are the typical challenges Managed UEM project teams face during each of the five process groups?

394. Why is it difficult to use Managed UEM project management software well?

395. Who will be the main sponsor for it?

396. Mass, power, cost ... why not time?

397. List five reasons why organizations outsource. Why is there a growing trend in outsourcing, especially in the government?

398. Are actual Managed UEM project results compared with planned or expected results to determine the variance?

399. How does Managed UEM project integration management relate to the Managed UEM project life cycle, stakeholders, and the other Managed UEM project management knowledge areas?

400. What are some crucial elements of a good Managed UEM project plan?

401. Which does one need in order to complete schedule development?

2.18 Duration Estimating Worksheet: Managed UEM

402. What info is needed?

403. Why estimate costs?

404. What is the total time required to complete the Managed UEM project if no delays occur?

405. How can the Managed UEM project be displayed graphically to better visualize the activities?

406. Define the work as completely as possible. What work will be included in the Managed UEM project?

407. When does your organization expect to be able to complete it?

408. Science = process: remember the scientific method?

409. When, then?

410. What utility impacts are there?

411. Small or large Managed UEM project?

412. Value pocket identification & quantification what are value pockets?

413. What are the critical bottleneck activities?

414. What is your role?

415. What is next?

416. Is the Managed UEM project responsive to community need?

417. How should ongoing costs be monitored to try to keep the Managed UEM project within budget?

418. Will the Managed UEM project collaborate with the local community and leverage resources?

419. Can the Managed UEM project be constructed as planned?

2.19 Project Schedule: Managed UEM

420. How can you address that situation?

421. Why is software Managed UEM project disaster so common?

422. Meet requirements?

423. How detailed should a Managed UEM project get?

424. Are the original Managed UEM project schedule and budget realistic?

425. Should you have a test for each code module?

426. Is infrastructure setup part of your Managed UEM project?

427. Did the Managed UEM project come in under budget?

428. Did the Managed UEM project come in on schedule?

429. Are procedures defined by which the Managed UEM project schedule may be changed?

430. It allows the Managed UEM project to be delivered on schedule. How Do you Use Schedules?

431. Have all Managed UEM project delays been adequately accounted for, communicated to all

stakeholders and adjustments made in overall Managed UEM project schedule?

432. Why do you need to manage Managed UEM project Risk?

433. What is the purpose of a Managed UEM project schedule?

434. Is there a Schedule Management Plan that establishes the criteria and activities for developing, monitoring and controlling the Managed UEM project schedule?

435. Why or why not?

436. Month Managed UEM project take?

437. How closely did the initial Managed UEM project Schedule compare with the actual schedule?

438. Why do you think schedule issues often cause the most conflicts on Managed UEM projects?

2.20 Cost Management Plan: Managed UEM

439. Is the schedule updated on a periodic basis?

440. Exclusions – is there scope to be performed or provided by others?

441. Managed UEM project definition & scope?

442. Does all Managed UEM project documentation reside in a common repository for easy access?

443. Is an industry recognized mechanized support tool(s) being used for Managed UEM project scheduling & tracking?

444. Scope of work – What is the likelihood and extent of potential future changes to the Managed UEM project scope?

445. Are tasks tracked by hours?

446. Is there anything unique in this Managed UEM projects scope statement that will affect resources?

447. Are the Managed UEM project plans updated on a frequent basis?

448. Is a stakeholder management plan in place that covers topics?

449. Are corrective actions and variances reported?

450. Milestones – what are the key dates in executing the contract plan?

451. Has the budget been baselined?

452. Does the detailed work plan match the complexity of tasks with the capabilities of personnel?

453. Are change requests logged and managed?

454. Have external dependencies been captured in the schedule?

455. What is Managed UEM project cost management?

456. Are staff skills known and available for each task?

457. Cost tracking and performance analysis – How will cost tracking and performance analysis be accomplished?

2.21 Activity Cost Estimates: Managed UEM

458. What is the Managed UEM projects sustainability strategy that will ensure Managed UEM project results will endure or be sustained?

459. How do you fund change orders?

460. How quickly can the task be done with the skills available?

461. How do you treat administrative costs in the activity inventory?

462. Was the consultant knowledgeable about the program?

463. How Award?

464. Who determines the quality and expertise of contractors?

465. What communication items need improvement?

466. How do you do activity recasts?

467. What is the estimators estimating history?

468. Scope statement only direct or indirect costs as well?

469. Is costing method consistent with study goals?

470. What is your organizations history in doing similar tasks?

471. Certification of actual expenditures?

472. Will you use any tools, such as Managed UEM project management software, to assist in capturing Earned Value metrics?

473. What is the activity inventory?

474. Based on your Managed UEM project communication management plan, what worked well?

475. Will you need to provide essential services information about activities?

476. The impact and what actions were taken?

2.22 Cost Estimating Worksheet: Managed UEM

477. Ask: are others positioned to know, are others credible, and will others cooperate?

478. Will the Managed UEM project collaborate with the local community and leverage resources?

479. Who is best positioned to know and assist in identifying corresponding factors?

480. Does the Managed UEM project provide innovative ways for stakeholders to overcome obstacles or deliver better outcomes?

481. What costs are to be estimated?

482. What will others want?

483. What is the estimated labor cost today based upon this information?

484. What happens to any remaining funds not used?

485. Is the Managed UEM project responsive to community need?

486. Can a trend be established from historical performance data on the selected measure and are the criteria for using trend analysis or forecasting methods met?

487. Identify the timeframe necessary to monitor progress and collect data to determine how the selected measure has changed?

488. What is the purpose of estimating?

489. How will the results be shared and to whom?

490. What can be included?

491. What additional Managed UEM project(s) could be initiated as a result of this Managed UEM project?

492. Is it feasible to establish a control group arrangement?

2.23 Cost Baseline: Managed UEM

493. How likely is it to go wrong?

494. What do you want to measure ?

495. Has the appropriate access to relevant data and analysis capability been granted?

496. Has the actual cost of the Managed UEM project (or Managed UEM project phase) been tallied and compared to the approved budget?

497. Is there anything you need from upper management in order to be successful?

498. Eac -estimate at completion, what is the total job expected to cost?

499. Is the requested change request a result of changes in other Managed UEM project(s)?

500. Why do you manage cost?

501. On budget?

502. What is the most important thing to do next to make your Managed UEM project successful?

503. Review your risk triggers -have your risks changed?

504. How concrete were original objectives?

505. How do you manage cost?

506. How will cost estimates be used?

507. What is the consequence?

508. When should cost estimates be developed?

509. Has the Managed UEM project (or Managed UEM project phase) been evaluated against each objective established in the product description and Integrated Managed UEM project Plan?

2.24 Quality Management Plan: Managed UEM

510. What would you gain if you spent time working to improve this process?

511. Do you periodically review your data quality system to see that it is up to date and appropriate?

512. Would impacts defined serve as impediments?

513. Were there any deficiencies / issues identified in the prior years self-assessment?

514. Does the system design reflect the requirements?

515. What does it do for you (or to me)?

516. What are your organizations current levels and trends for the already stated measures related to customer satisfaction/ dissatisfaction and product/ service performance?

517. How does your organization manage training and evaluate its effectiveness?

518. Is this a Requirement?

519. Does a documented Managed UEM project organizational policy & plan (i.e. governance model) exist?

520. Are you following the quality standards?

521. Do you keep back-up copies of any data?

522. How do your action plans support the strategic objectives?

523. Written by multiple authors and in multiple writing styles?

524. What process do you use to minimize errors, defects, and rework?

525. How are calibration records kept?

526. After observing execution of process, is it in compliance with the documented Plan?

527. How is equipment calibrated?

528. How are corresponding standards measured?

2.25 Quality Metrics: Managed UEM

529. What can manufacturing professionals do to ensure quality is seen as an integral part of the entire product lifecycle?

530. What approved evidence based screening tools can be used?

531. Is there alignment within your organization on definitions?

532. Is material complete (and does it meet the standards)?

533. If the defect rate during testing is substantially higher than that of the previous release (or a similar product), then ask: Did you plan for and actually improve testing effectiveness?

534. How do you know if everyone is trying to improve the right things?

535. What happens if you get an abnormal result?

536. Are there any open risk issues?

537. How do you communicate results and findings to upper management?

538. Why is now the time for quality metrics?

539. What about still open problems?

540. Were quality attributes reported?

541. How do you measure?

542. Is quality culture a competitive advantage?

543. Which are the right metrics to use?

544. What makes a visualization memorable?

545. Did evaluation start on time?

546. Subjective quality component: customer satisfaction, how do you measure it?

547. Is the reporting frequency appropriate?

548. What metrics do you measure?

2.26 Process Improvement Plan: Managed UEM

549. Everyone agrees on what process improvement is, right?

550. What personnel are the sponsors for that initiative?

551. What is quality and how will you ensure it?

552. Where are you now?

553. Where do you want to be?

554. What makes people good SPI coaches?

555. Does explicit definition of the measures exist?

556. Are you meeting the quality standards?

557. Are you making progress on the goals?

558. Are there forms and procedures to collect and record the data?

559. What is the test-cycle concept?

560. Why quality management?

561. To elicit goal statements, do you ask a question such as, What do you want to achieve?

562. Have the supporting tools been developed or acquired?

563. What lessons have you learned so far?

564. Has the time line required to move measurement results from the points of collection to databases or users been established?

565. Modeling current processes is great, and will you ever see a return on that investment?

566. Has a process guide to collect the data been developed?

567. What is the return on investment?

2.27 Responsibility Assignment Matrix: Managed UEM

568. Undistributed budgets, if any?

569. What will the work cost?

570. Budgeted cost for work performed?

571. Are the wbs and organizational levels for application of the Managed UEM projected overhead costs identified?

572. Do others have the time to dedicate to your Managed UEM project?

573. Are there any drawbacks to using a responsibility assignment matrix?

574. Changes in the nature of the overhead requirements?

575. Are the actual costs used for variance analysis reconcilable with data from the accounting system?

576. Are management actions taken to reduce indirect costs when there are significant adverse variances?

577. The staff interests – is the group or the person interested in working for this Managed UEM project?

578. Is budgeted cost for work performed calculated

in a manner consistent with the way work is planned?

579. Does the Managed UEM project need to be analyzed further to uncover additional responsibilities?

580. Are all authorized tasks assigned to identified organizational elements?

581. Are detailed work packages planned as far in advance as practicable?

582. Identify potential or actual budget-based and time-based schedule variances?

583. What is the primary purpose of the human resource plan?

2.28 Roles and Responsibilities: Managed UEM

584. Be specific; avoid generalities. Thank you and great work alone are insufficient. What exactly do you appreciate and why?

585. Was the expectation clearly communicated?

586. Does the team have access to and ability to use data analysis tools?

587. What expectations were NOT met?

588. What should you highlight for improvement?

589. Is the data complete?

590. What specific behaviors did you observe?

591. Is there a training program in place for stakeholders covering expectations, roles and responsibilities and any addition knowledge others need to be good stakeholders?

592. What is working well?

593. What should you do now to ensure that you are meeting all expectations of your current position?

594. What areas of supervision are challenging for you?

595. Where are you most strong as a supervisor?

596. Who is responsible for implementation activities and where will the functions, roles and responsibilities be defined?

597. Are governance roles and responsibilities documented?

598. What should you do now to prepare for your career 5+ years from now?

599. Do you take the time to clearly define roles and responsibilities on Managed UEM project tasks?

600. Required skills, knowledge, experience?

601. Who is responsible for each task?

2.29 Human Resource Management Plan: Managed UEM

602. Is there a Quality Management Plan?

603. Have Managed UEM project success criteria been defined?

604. How complete is the human resource management plan?

605. Are people motivated to meet the current and future challenges?

606. Has a sponsor been identified?

607. Has a structured approach been used to break work effort into manageable components (WBS)?

608. Timeline and milestones?

609. Is there a formal process for updating the Managed UEM project baseline?

610. Do Managed UEM project managers participating in the Managed UEM project know the Managed UEM projects true status first hand?

611. Are people being developed to meet the challenges of the future?

612. Have the key elements of a coherent Managed UEM project management strategy been established?

613. Are post milestone Managed UEM project reviews (PMPR) conducted with your organization at least once a year?

614. Is the steering committee active in Managed UEM project oversight?

615. Is your organization human?

616. Does the schedule include Managed UEM project management time and change request analysis time?

617. Has the schedule been baselined?

618. How are superior performers differentiated from average performers?

619. Are multiple estimation methods being employed?

2.30 Communications Management Plan: Managed UEM

620. Are there too many who have an interest in some aspect of your work?

621. What help do you and your team need from the stakeholder?

622. Are others part of the communications management plan?

623. Who will use or be affected by the result of a Managed UEM project?

624. Who are the members of the governing body?

625. Why do you manage communications?

626. Who did you turn to if you had questions?

627. Why is stakeholder engagement important?

628. How often do you engage with stakeholders?

629. What is the political influence?

630. Timing: when do the effects of the communication take place?

631. Are you constantly rushing from meeting to meeting?

632. What to learn?

633. Do you have members of your team responsible for certain stakeholders?

634. What are the interrelationships?

635. Which team member will work with each stakeholder?

636. What does the stakeholder need from the team?

637. What is the stakeholders level of authority?

638. Is the stakeholder role recognized by your organization?

639. Will messages be directly related to the release strategy or phases of the Managed UEM project?

2.31 Risk Management Plan: Managed UEM

640. Are tool mentors available?

641. Who/what can assist?

642. How quickly does each item need to be resolved?

643. What can go wrong?

644. How do you manage Managed UEM project Risk?

645. How can the process be made more effective or less cumbersome (process improvements)?

646. For software; are compilers and code generators available and suitable for the product to be built?

647. Risk may be made during which step of risk management?

648. What should be done with non-critical risks?

649. Who should be notified of the occurrence of each of the indicators?

650. Why might it be late?

651. What is the likelihood that your organization would accept responsibility for the risk?

652. Should the risk be taken at all?

653. Where do risks appear in the business phases?

654. Which risks should get the attention?

655. Can the risk be avoided by choosing a different alternative?

656. Can it be changed quickly?

657. Has something like this been done before?

658. Can the Managed UEM project proceed without assuming the risk?

659. Have you worked with the customer in the past?

2.32 Risk Register: Managed UEM

660. Manageability – have mitigations to the risk been identified?

661. What is the probability and impact of the risk occurring?

662. Are there any knock-on effects/impact on any of the other areas?

663. What will be done?

664. Are corrective measures implemented as planned?

665. When would you develop a risk register?

666. Contingency actions - planned actions to reduce the immediate seriousness of the risk when it does occur. What should you do when?

667. Risk documentation: what reporting formats and processes will be used for risk management activities?

668. Have other controls and solutions been implemented in other services which could be applied as an alternative to additional funding?

669. What can be done about it?

670. What is a Community Risk Register?

671. Are your objectives at risk?

672. Does the evidence highlight any areas to advance opportunities or foster good relations. If yes what steps will be taken?

673. How could corresponding Risk affect the Managed UEM project in terms of cost and schedule?

674. What is the appropriate level of risk management for this Managed UEM project?

675. What are the major risks facing the Managed UEM project?

676. People risk -are people with appropriate skills available to help complete the Managed UEM project?

677. What evidence do you have to justify the likelihood score of the risk (audit, incident report, claim, complaints, inspection, internal review)?

678. How is a Community Risk Register created?

2.33 Probability and Impact Assessment: Managed UEM

679. Would avoiding any of corresponding impact the Managed UEM projects chance of success?

680. What is the likelihood?

681. Is the customer technically sophisticated in the product area?

682. Are end-users enthusiastically committed to the Managed UEM project and the system/product to be built?

683. Is a software Managed UEM project management tool available?

684. What are the current demands of the customer?

685. Assuming that you have identified a number of risks in the Managed UEM project, how would you prioritize them?

686. Has the need for the Managed UEM project been properly established?

687. Is the present organizational structure for handling the Managed UEM project sufficient?

688. What is the Managed UEM project managers level of commitment and professionalism?

689. Are people attending meetings and doing work?

690. What risks does your organization have if the Managed UEM projects fail to meet deadline?

691. What is the risk appetite?

692. How risk averse are you?

693. Are Managed UEM project requirements stable?

694. How is risk handled within this Managed UEM project organization?

695. Are testing tools available and suitable?

696. Are the risk data timely and relevant?

697. Do you use any methods to analyze risks?

2.34 Probability and Impact Matrix: Managed UEM

698. Is the present organizational structure for handling the Managed UEM project sufficient?

699. Which role do you have in the Managed UEM project?

700. Do the requirements require the creation of new algorithms?

701. Can it be enlarged by drawing people from other areas of your organization?

702. What is Managed UEM project risk management?

703. Is a software Managed UEM project management tool available?

704. How well is the risk understood?

705. How solid is the Managed UEM projection of competitive reaction?

706. Have staff received necessary training?

707. How to prioritize risks?

708. What are the likely future requirements?

709. What has the Managed UEM project manager forgotten to do?

710. Are the risk data complete?

711. What would be the best solution?

712. What should be the gestation period for the Managed UEM project with this technology?

713. During Managed UEM project executing, a team member identifies a risk that is not in the risk register. What should you do?

714. Which of your Managed UEM projects should be selected when compared with other Managed UEM projects?

2.35 Risk Data Sheet: Managed UEM

715. What will be the consequences if the risk happens?

716. How do you handle product safely?

717. What do people affected think about the need for, and practicality of preventive measures?

718. How can hazards be reduced?

719. What are the main opportunities available to you that you should grab while you can?

720. What actions can be taken to eliminate or remove risk?

721. Type of risk identified?

722. Whom do you serve (customers)?

723. What do you know?

724. What are your core values?

725. Potential for recurrence?

726. During work activities could hazards exist?

727. What is the environment within which you operate (social trends, economic, community values, broad based participation, national directions etc.)?

728. What if client refuses?

729. What can you do?

730. What are you weak at and therefore need to do better?

731. Who has a vested interest in how you perform as your organization (our stakeholders)?

732. What are you trying to achieve (Objectives)?

733. What are you here for (Mission)?

2.36 Procurement Management Plan: Managed UEM

734. Has the Managed UEM project scope been baselined?

735. Are non-critical path items updated and agreed upon with the teams?

736. Is the steering committee active in Managed UEM project oversight?

737. Public engagement – did you get it right?

738. Are Managed UEM project team members committed fulltime?

739. Are Managed UEM project contact logs kept up to date?

740. What were things that you did well, and could improve, and how?

741. How long will it take for the purchase cost to be the same as the lease cost?

742. Are quality metrics defined?

743. Are the appropriate IT resources adequate to meet planned commitments?

744. Similar Managed UEM projects?

745. Has Managed UEM project success criteria been defined?

746. Alignment to strategic goals & objectives?

747. Have the key elements of a coherent Managed UEM project management strategy been established?

748. How will the duration of the Managed UEM project influence your decisions?

749. Are parking lot items captured?

750. Are updated Managed UEM project time & resource estimates reasonable based on the current Managed UEM project stage?

2.37 Source Selection Criteria: Managed UEM

751. Are there any common areas of weaknesses or deficiencies in the proposals in the competitive range?

752. Do you want to have them collaborate at subfactor level?

753. What documentation is needed for a tradeoff decision?

754. What is price analysis and when should it be performed?

755. How is past performance evaluated?

756. What should communications be used to accomplish?

757. In order of importance, which evaluation criteria are the most critical to the determination of your overall rating?

758. How organization are proposed quotes/prices?

759. Which contract type places the most risk on the seller?

760. How can business terms and conditions be improved to yield more effective price competition?

761. What instructions should be provided regarding oral presentations?

762. How much past performance information should be requested?

763. What are the most critical evaluation criteria that prove to be tiebreakers in the evaluation of proposals?

764. How are clarifications and communications appropriately used?

765. Is experience evaluated?

766. Is a letter of commitment from each proposed team member and key subcontractor included?

767. What past performance information should be requested?

768. What are the requirements for publicizing a RFP?

769. How much weight should be placed on past performance information?

770. What will you use to capture evaluation and subsequent documentation?

2.38 Stakeholder Management Plan: Managed UEM

771. Who is responsible for gathering and reporting data for employment?

772. Does the business case include how the Managed UEM project aligns with your organizations strategic goals & objectives?

773. Are enough systems & user personnel assigned to the Managed UEM project?

774. What is meant by activity dependencies and how do they relate to network diagramming?

775. Are target dates established for each milestone deliverable?

776. Does the Managed UEM project have a Statement of Work?

777. Are Managed UEM project contact logs kept up to date?

778. How will the equipment be verified?

779. Is pert / critical path or equivalent methodology being used?

780. Does the resource management plan include a personnel development plan?

781. Where are the verification requirements to be documented (eg purchase order, agreement etc)?

782. Does the Managed UEM project have a Quality Culture?

783. Are the quality tools and methods identified in the Quality Plan appropriate to the Managed UEM project?

784. What is the general purpose in defining responsibilities of the already stated affiliated with the Managed UEM project?

2.39 Change Management Plan: Managed UEM

785. What new competencies will be required for the roles?

786. How far reaching in your organization is the change?

787. How much Managed UEM project management is needed?

788. Would you need to tailor a special message for each segment of the audience?

789. What are the major changes to processes?

790. Is it the same for each of the business units?

791. How can you best frame the message so that it addresses the audiences interests?

792. Who will do the training?

793. What risks may occur upfront?

794. Has a training need analysis been carried out?

795. What work practices will be affected?

796. Has the priority for this Managed UEM project been set by the Business Unit Management Team?

797. What are the specific target groups / audience that will be impacted by this change?

798. Are work location changes required?

799. What are the needs, priorities and special interests of the audience?

800. Has an information & communications plan been developed?

801. Have the business unit contacts been briefed by the Managed UEM project team?

802. Are there resource implications for your communications strategy?

803. Who will be the change levers?

3.0 Executing Process Group: Managed UEM

804. What are deliverables of your Managed UEM project?

805. What Managed UEM projects and services are in the portfolio of your organization?

806. Were sponsors and decision makers available when needed outside regularly scheduled meetings?

807. In what way has the program come up with innovative measures for problem-solving?

808. What is the critical path for this Managed UEM project and how long is it?

809. What type of information goes in the quality assurance plan?

810. Just how important is your work to the overall success of the Managed UEM project?

811. What are the key components of the Managed UEM project communications plan?

812. What are the challenges Managed UEM project teams face?

813. When is the appropriate time to bring the scorecard to Board meetings?

814. What are the main types of goods and services being outsourced?

815. Measurable - are the targets measurable?

816. How well defined and documented were the Managed UEM project management processes you chose to use?

817. How many different communication channels does the Managed UEM project team have?

818. What does it mean to take a systems view of a Managed UEM project?

819. Will a new application be developed using existing hardware, software, and networks?

820. Is the Managed UEM project making progress in helping to achieve the set results?

3.1 Team Member Status Report: Managed UEM

821. Are your organizations Managed UEM projects more successful over time?

822. What specific interest groups do you have in place?

823. When a teams productivity and success depend on collaboration and the efficient flow of information, what generally fails them?

824. Is there evidence that staff is taking a more professional approach toward management of your organizations Managed UEM projects?

825. The problem with Reward & Recognition Programs is that the truly deserving people all too often get left out. How can you make it practical?

826. Will the staff do training or is that done by a third party?

827. How it is to be done?

828. Are the products of your organizations Managed UEM projects meeting customers objectives?

829. How much risk is involved?

830. Do you have an Enterprise Managed UEM project Management Office (EPMO)?

831. How will resource planning be done?

832. How does this product, good, or service meet the needs of the Managed UEM project and your organization as a whole?

833. How can you make it practical?

834. Does your organization have the means (staff, money, contract, etc.) to produce or to acquire the product, good, or service?

835. Why is it to be done?

836. Are the attitudes of staff regarding Managed UEM project work improving?

837. Does every department have to have a Managed UEM project Manager on staff?

838. Does the product, good, or service already exist within your organization?

839. What is to be done?

3.2 Change Request: Managed UEM

840. What is the relationship between requirements attributes and attributes like complexity and size?

841. What is the change request log?

842. How is the change documented (format, content, storage)?

843. Who is included in the change control team?

844. What are the requirements for urgent changes?

845. When to submit a change request?

846. Will the change use memory to the extent that other functions will be not have sufficient memory to operate effectively?

847. How well do experienced software developers predict software change?

848. Will this change conflict with other requirements changes (e.g., lead to conflicting operational scenarios)?

849. How are the measures for carrying out the change established?

850. Is it feasible to use requirements attributes as predictors of reliability?

851. How many lines of code must be changed to

implement the change?

852. What is the relationship between requirements attributes and reliability?

853. Will there be a change request form in use?

854. How do team members communicate with each other?

855. How to get changes (code) out in a timely manner?

856. How shall the implementation of changes be recorded?

857. What mechanism is used to appraise others of changes that are made?

858. Who is responsible to authorize changes?

3.3 Change Log: Managed UEM

859. Who initiated the change request?

860. Is the change request within Managed UEM project scope?

861. Should a more thorough impact analysis be conducted?

862. Is the submitted change a new change or a modification of a previously approved change?

863. When was the request approved?

864. Does the suggested change request seem to represent a necessary enhancement to the product?

865. How does this relate to the standards developed for specific business processes?

866. How does this change affect the timeline of the schedule?

867. Does the suggested change request represent a desired enhancement to the products functionality?

868. Is the requested change request a result of changes in other Managed UEM project(s)?

869. Is this a mandatory replacement?

870. Do the described changes impact on the integrity or security of the system?

871. Will the Managed UEM project fail if the change request is not executed?

872. Is the change backward compatible without limitations?

873. When was the request submitted?

874. Is the change request open, closed or pending?

875. Where do changes come from?

876. How does this change affect scope?

3.4 Decision Log: Managed UEM

877. How do you know when you are achieving it?

878. Decision-making process; how will the team make decisions?

879. At what point in time does loss become unacceptable?

880. How does an increasing emphasis on cost containment influence the strategies and tactics used?

881. Which variables make a critical difference?

882. Meeting purpose; why does this team meet?

883. How does provision of information, both in terms of content and presentation, influence acceptance of alternative strategies?

884. Who is the decisionmaker?

885. How consolidated and comprehensive a story can you tell by capturing currently available incident data in a central location and through a log of key decisions during an incident?

886. Who will be given a copy of this document and where will it be kept?

887. What is the average size of your matters in an applicable measurement?

888. What eDiscovery problem or issue did your organization set out to fix or make better?

889. Do strategies and tactics aimed at less than full control reduce the costs of management or simply shift the cost burden?

890. Is your opponent open to a non-traditional workflow, or will it likely challenge anything you do?

891. Adversarial environment. is your opponent open to a non-traditional workflow, or will it likely challenge anything you do?

892. What was the rationale for the decision?

893. With whom was the decision shared or considered?

894. How does the use a Decision Support System influence the strategies/tactics or costs?

895. Does anything need to be adjusted?

896. What is the line where eDiscovery ends and document review begins?

3.5 Quality Audit: Managed UEM

897. How does your organization know that it is maintaining a conducive staff climate?

898. How does your organization know that the quality of its supervisors is appropriately effective and constructive?

899. Do all staff have the necessary authority and resources to deliver what is expected of them?

900. How does your organization know that it is appropriately effective and constructive in preparing its staff for organizational aspirations?

901. How does your organization know that its systems for assisting staff with career planning and employment placements are appropriately effective and constructive?

902. How does your organization know that its system for supporting staff research capability is appropriately effective and constructive?

903. Does the report read coherently?

904. How does your organization know that its systems for communicating with and among staff are appropriately effective and constructive?

905. How does your organization know that its planning processes are appropriately effective and constructive?

906. Are storage areas and reconditioning operations designed to prevent mix-ups and assure orderly handling of both the distressed and reconditioned devices?

907. Is there a written corporate quality policy?

908. Are there appropriate indicators for monitoring the effectiveness and efficiency of processes?

909. How does your organization know that its research programs are appropriately effective and constructive?

910. Is your organizations resource allocation system properly aligned with its collection of intentions?

911. It is inappropriate to seek information about the Audit Panels preliminary views including questions like why do you ask that?

912. Do the suppliers use a formal quality system?

913. How does your organization know that its staff are presenting original work, and properly acknowledging the work of others?

914. What experience do staff have in the type of work that the audit entails?

915. How does your organization know that its system for ensuring a positive organizational climate is appropriately effective and constructive?

916. How does your organization know that its

system for inducting new staff to maximize workplace contributions are appropriately effective and constructive?

3.6 Team Directory: Managed UEM

917. Process decisions: are contractors adequately prosecuting the work?

918. How and in what format should information be presented?

919. How will you accomplish and manage the objectives?

920. Process decisions: how well was task order work performed?

921. Process decisions: do job conditions warrant additional actions to collect job information and document on-site activity?

922. Who is the Sponsor?

923. Who are the Team Members?

924. Who are your stakeholders (customers, sponsors, end users, team members)?

925. What are you going to deliver or accomplish?

926. Is construction on schedule?

927. What needs to be communicated?

928. Process decisions: is work progressing on schedule and per contract requirements?

929. Timing: when do the effects of communication take place?

930. How will the team handle changes?

931. Who will be the stakeholders on your next Managed UEM project?

932. Who will write the meeting minutes and distribute?

933. Who will talk to the customer?

934. Decisions: what could be done better to improve the quality of the constructed product?

935. When does information need to be distributed?

3.7 Team Operating Agreement: Managed UEM

936. Do you record meetings for the already stated unable to attend?

937. How will you divide work equitably?

938. Do you determine the meeting length and time of day?

939. To whom do you deliver your services?

940. Must your members collaborate successfully to complete Managed UEM projects?

941. Have you established procedures that team members can follow to work effectively together, such as a team operating agreement?

942. Resource allocation: how will individual team members account for time and expenses, and how will this be allocated in the team budget?

943. Conflict resolution: how will disputes and other conflicts be mediated or resolved?

944. What is teaming?

945. Do you brief absent members after they view meeting notes or listen to a recording?

946. Have you set the goals and objectives of the

team?

947. Do you call or email participants to ensure understanding, follow-through and commitment to the meeting outcomes?

948. What are the safety issues/risks that need to be addressed and/or that the team needs to consider?

949. What are the boundaries (organizational or geographic) within which you operate?

950. Do you send out the agenda and meeting materials in advance?

951. Do team members reside in more than two countries?

952. What is the number of cases currently teamed?

953. Do you ensure that all participants know how to use the required technology?

954. Are there more than two native languages represented by your team?

3.8 Team Performance Assessment: Managed UEM

955. To what degree can the team measure progress against specific goals?

956. To what degree does the teams purpose constitute a broader, deeper aspiration than just accomplishing short-term goals?

957. How do you manage human resources?

958. Social categorization and intergroup behaviour: Does minimal intergroup discrimination make social identity more positive?

959. What are you doing specifically to develop the leaders around you?

960. If you have received criticism from reviewers that your work suffered from method variance, what was the circumstance?

961. To what degree do team members articulate the teams work approach?

962. To what degree will the team ensure that all members equitably share the work essential to the success of the team?

963. To what degree do the goals specify concrete team work products?

964. To what degree do team members understand one anothers roles and skills?

965. To what degree does the teams work approach provide opportunity for members to engage in open interaction?

966. Where to from here?

967. Lack of method variance in self-reported affect and perceptions at work: Reality or artifact?

968. Which situations call for a more extreme type of adaptiveness in which team members actually re-define roles?

969. What is method variance?

970. To what degree are staff involved as partners in the improvement process?

971. To what degree will the team adopt a concrete, clearly understood, and agreed-upon approach that will result in achievement of the teams goals?

972. Do you promptly inform members about major developments that may affect them?

973. To what degree are the teams goals and objectives clear, simple, and measurable?

974. To what degree can team members frequently and easily communicate with one another?

3.9 Team Member Performance Assessment: Managed UEM

975. What types of learning are targeted (e.g., cognitive, affective, psychomotor, procedural)?

976. How are performance measures and associated incentives developed?

977. How do you currently use the time that is available?

978. What is collaboration?

979. What evidence supports your decision-making?

980. To what degree is the team cognizant of small wins to be celebrated along the way?

981. New skills/knowledge gained this year?

982. To what extent did the evaluation influence the instructional path, such as with adaptive testing?

983. Is it critical or vital to the job?

984. How do you start collaborating?

985. To what degree do team members frequently explore the teams purpose and its implications?

986. How is assessment information achieved, stored?

987. What is the Business Management Oversight Process?

988. How do you use data to inform instruction and improve staff achievement?

989. To what degree does the teams purpose contain themes that are particularly meaningful and memorable?

990. What are top priorities?

991. Are assessment validation activities performed?

3.10 Issue Log: Managed UEM

992. What approaches do you use?

993. Who is involved as you identify stakeholders?

994. Who were proponents/opponents?

995. How were past initiatives successful?

996. In your work, how much time is spent on stakeholder identification?

997. What steps can you take for positive relationships?

998. What is the status of the issue?

999. Can an impact cause deviation beyond team, stage or Managed UEM project tolerances?

1000. What is a Stakeholder?

1001. Is access to the Issue Log controlled?

1002. Is the issue log kept in a safe place?

1003. Do you often overlook a key stakeholder or stakeholder group?

1004. Do you prepare stakeholder engagement plans?

1005. What date was the issue resolved?

1006. What is the impact on the risks?

1007. Who is the issue assigned to?

1008. How is this initiative related to other portfolios, programs, or Managed UEM projects?

4.0 Monitoring and Controlling Process Group: Managed UEM

1009. When will the Managed UEM project be done?

1010. How do you monitor progress?

1011. Who needs to be involved in the planning?

1012. Is the program making progress in helping to achieve the set results?

1013. How well defined and documented were the Managed UEM project management processes you chose to use?

1014. Overall, how does the program function to serve the clients?

1015. Purpose: toward what end is the evaluation being conducted?

1016. What input will you be required to provide the Managed UEM project team?

1017. Is progress on outcomes due to your program?

1018. User: who wants the information and what are they interested in?

1019. What is the timeline?

1020. Is there adequate validation on required fields?

1021. Are the services being delivered?

1022. Do the products created live up to the necessary quality?

1023. Is the verbiage used appropriate and understandable?

1024. Did it work?

1025. What business situation is being addressed?

1026. Is there sufficient funding available for this?

4.1 Project Performance Report: Managed UEM

1027. To what degree are the tasks requirements reflected in the flow and storage of information?

1028. To what degree do the relationships of the informal organization motivate taskrelevant behavior and facilitate task completion?

1029. What is the PRS?

1030. To what degree does the teams approach to its work allow for modification and improvement over time?

1031. To what degree will the approach capitalize on and enhance the skills of all team members in a manner that takes into consideration other demands on members of the team?

1032. To what degree do team members feel that the purpose of the team is important, if not exciting?

1033. To what degree does the formal organization make use of individual resources and meet individual needs?

1034. To what degree do all members feel responsible for all agreed-upon measures?

1035. To what degree does the team possess adequate membership to achieve its ends?

1036. What is the degree to which rules govern information exchange between groups?

1037. What degree are the relative importance and priority of the goals clear to all team members?

1038. To what degree are the skill areas critical to team performance present?

1039. To what degree are the demands of the task compatible with and converge with the mission and functions of the formal organization?

1040. To what degree do the structures of the formal organization motivate taskrelevant behavior and facilitate task completion?

4.2 Variance Analysis: Managed UEM

1041. How do you manage changes in the nature of the overhead requirements?

1042. How do you verify authorization to proceed with all authorized work?

1043. Do the rates and prices remain constant throughout the year?

1044. Are material costs reported within the same period as that in which BCWP is earned for that material?

1045. Are procedures for variance analysis documented and consistently applied at the control account level and selected WBS and organizational levels at least monthly as a routine task?

1046. What are the direct labor dollars and/or hours?

1047. What is the performance to date and material commitment?

1048. Are the wbs and organizational levels for application of the Managed UEM projected overhead costs identified?

1049. What business event caused the fluctuation?

1050. Are control accounts opened and closed based on the start and completion of work contained therein?

1051. How are material, labor, and overhead variances calculated and recorded?

1052. Who is generally responsible for monitoring and taking action on variances?

1053. Are the overhead pools formally and adequately identified?

1054. Are authorized changes being incorporated in a timely manner?

1055. Are there changes in the overhead pool and/or organization structures?

1056. When, during the last four quarters, did a primary business event occur causing a fluctuation?

1057. Can the relationship with problem customers be restructured so that there is a win-win situation?

4.3 Earned Value Status: Managed UEM

1058. Are you hitting your Managed UEM projects targets?

1059. Verification is a process of ensuring that the developed system satisfies the stakeholders agreements and specifications; Are you building the product right? What do you verify?

1060. How does this compare with other Managed UEM projects?

1061. Earned value can be used in almost any Managed UEM project situation and in almost any Managed UEM project environment. it may be used on large Managed UEM projects, medium sized Managed UEM projects, tiny Managed UEM projects (in cut-down form), complex and simple Managed UEM projects and in any market sector. some people, of course, know all about earned value, they have used it for years - but perhaps not as effectively as they could have?

1062. How much is it going to cost by the finish?

1063. What is the unit of forecast value?

1064. If earned value management (EVM) is so good in determining the true status of a Managed UEM project and Managed UEM project its completion, why is it that hardly any one uses it in information systems related Managed UEM projects?

1065. Validation is a process of ensuring that the developed system will actually achieve the stakeholders desired outcomes; Are you building the right product? What do you validate?

1066. Where is evidence-based earned value in your organization reported?

1067. Where are your problem areas?

1068. When is it going to finish?

4.4 Risk Audit: Managed UEM

1069. Can assurance be expanded beyond the traditional audit without undermining independence?

1070. Do you promote education and training opportunities?

1071. Does the Managed UEM project team have experience with the technology to be implemented?

1072. If applicable; which route/packaging option do you choose for transport of hazmat material?

1073. Are all participants informed of safety issues?

1074. What effect would a better risk management program have had?

1075. Does your organization have a process for meeting its ongoing taxation obligations?

1076. Do you have a realistic budget and do you present regular financial reports that identify how you are going against that budget?

1077. Does your board meet regularly and document all decisions and actions?

1078. Auditor independence: a burdensome constraint or a core value?

1079. Have all possible risks/hazards been identified (including injury to staff, damage to equipment, impact on others in the community)?

1080. Do you have a consistent repeatable process that is actually used?

1081. Are the best people available?

1082. Are all managers or operators of the facility or equipment competent or qualified?

1083. Is the number of people on the Managed UEM project team adequate to do the job?

1084. Is your organization willing to commit significant time to the requirements gathering process?

1085. How effective are your risk controls?

1086. Are corresponding safety and risk management policies posted for all to see?

1087. Have reasonable steps been taken to reduce the risks to acceptable levels?

1088. Does the implementation method matter?

4.5 Contractor Status Report: Managed UEM

1089. How is risk transferred?

1090. Describe how often regular updates are made to the proposed solution. Are corresponding regular updates included in the standard maintenance plan?

1091. Who can list a Managed UEM project as organization experience, your organization or a previous employee of your organization?

1092. What is the average response time for answering a support call?

1093. How long have you been using the services?

1094. What was the final actual cost?

1095. What was the overall budget or estimated cost?

1096. What are the minimum and optimal bandwidth requirements for the proposed solution?

1097. Are there contractual transfer concerns?

1098. What process manages the contracts?

1099. What was the budget or estimated cost for your organizations services?

1100. What was the actual budget or estimated cost

for your organizations services?

1101. How does the proposed individual meet each requirement?

1102. If applicable; describe your standard schedule for new software version releases. Are new software version releases included in the standard maintenance plan?

4.6 Formal Acceptance: Managed UEM

1103. What features, practices, and processes proved to be strengths or weaknesses?

1104. Does it do what client said it would?

1105. Is formal acceptance of the Managed UEM project product documented and distributed?

1106. Was the sponsor/customer satisfied?

1107. Have all comments been addressed?

1108. Was the Managed UEM project managed well?

1109. What lessons were learned about your Managed UEM project management methodology?

1110. General estimate of the costs and times to complete the Managed UEM project?

1111. Was the Managed UEM project goal achieved?

1112. Does it do what Managed UEM project team said it would?

1113. How does your team plan to obtain formal acceptance on your Managed UEM project?

1114. What was done right?

1115. Did the Managed UEM project achieve its MOV?

1116. Do you perform formal acceptance or burn-in tests?

1117. How well did the team follow the methodology?

1118. Did the Managed UEM project manager and team act in a professional and ethical manner?

1119. Who supplies data?

1120. Was the Managed UEM project work done on time, within budget, and according to specification?

1121. What function(s) does it fill or meet?

1122. What is the Acceptance Management Process?

5.0 Closing Process Group: Managed UEM

1123. What is an Encumbrance?

1124. Was the user/client satisfied with the end product?

1125. Is the Managed UEM project funded?

1126. Were risks identified and mitigated?

1127. When will the Managed UEM project be done?

1128. What will you do to minimize the impact should a risk event occur?

1129. What areas were overlooked on this Managed UEM project?

1130. How dependent is the Managed UEM project on other Managed UEM projects or work efforts?

1131. How well did you do?

1132. Did you do what you said you were going to do?

1133. How well did the chosen processes fit the needs of the Managed UEM project?

1134. Was the schedule met?

1135. What is the overall risk of the Managed UEM

project to your organization?

1136. What was learned?

1137. How well defined and documented were the Managed UEM project management processes you chose to use?

5.1 Procurement Audit: Managed UEM

1138. Was there reasonable justification for the need of the purchase, namely when made towards the end of the financial year?

1139. Was invitation to tender to each specific contract issued after the evaluation of the indicative tenders was completed?

1140. If an electronic auction or a dynamic purchasing system was used, did the tender documents specify details on access to information, electronic equipment used and connection specifications?

1141. Are open purchase orders with a fixed monetary limitation used for local purchases of small dollar value?

1142. Are services/tasks combined in such a way that the market is used where relevant?

1143. Are buyers rotated so that they do not deal with the same vendors year in and year out?

1144. Is there a system in place to handle partial delivery of orders, back orders, and partial payments?

1145. Are risks in the external environment identified, for example: Budgetary constraints?

1146. Are all pre-numbered checks accounted for on a

regular basis?

1147. Are the pages of the minutes book press pre-numbered?

1148. Are there appropriate controls in place to ensure that the procurement Managed UEM project complies with relevant legislation?

1149. Are rules in automatic disbursement programs adequate to prevent duplicate payment of invoices?

1150. Are unusual uses of organization funds investigated?

1151. Have the funding arrangements been agreed where payments take place over several financial periods?

1152. Is it assessed whether well-functioning markets exist for the departments services/tasks?

1153. Are all purchase orders cancelled after payment to avoid duplicate payment of the same invoice?

1154. Has your organization procedures in place to monitor the input of experts employed to assist the procurement function?

1155. Has your organization clearly defined the award criteria?

1156. Is trend analysis performed on expenditures made by key employees and by vendor?

1157. Are staff members evaluated in accordance with

the terms of existing negotiated agreements?

5.2 Contract Close-Out: Managed UEM

1158. Have all contracts been closed?

1159. How/when used ?

1160. What happens to the recipient of services?

1161. How does it work?

1162. Have all acceptance criteria been met prior to final payment to contractors?

1163. Have all contract records been included in the Managed UEM project archives?

1164. Are the signers the authorized officials?

1165. Was the contract sufficiently clear so as not to result in numerous disputes and misunderstandings?

1166. Change in knowledge?

1167. Has each contract been audited to verify acceptance and delivery?

1168. Was the contract complete without requiring numerous changes and revisions?

1169. How is the contracting office notified of the automatic contract close-out?

1170. What is capture management?

1171. Change in attitude or behavior?

1172. Was the contract type appropriate?

1173. Have all contracts been completed?

1174. Why Outsource?

1175. Change in circumstances?

1176. Parties: Authorized?

1177. Parties: who is involved?

5.3 Project or Phase Close-Out: Managed UEM

1178. What information is each stakeholder group interested in?

1179. What security considerations needed to be addressed during the procurement life cycle?

1180. What process was planned for managing issues/risks?

1181. What were the desired outcomes?

1182. Which changes might a stakeholder be required to make as a result of the Managed UEM project?

1183. Were the outcomes different from the already stated planned?

1184. If you were the Managed UEM project sponsor, how would you determine which Managed UEM project team(s) and/or individuals deserve recognition?

1185. What are they?

1186. Planned completion date?

1187. When and how were information needs best met?

1188. What is the information level of detail required

for each stakeholder?

1189. Can the lesson learned be replicated?

1190. What advantages do the an individual interview have over a group meeting, and vice-versa?

1191. Does the lesson describe a function that would be done differently the next time?

1192. Did the delivered product meet the specified requirements and goals of the Managed UEM project?

1193. What could be done to improve the process?

1194. What is this stakeholder expecting?

1195. Have business partners been involved extensively, and what data was required for them?

5.4 Lessons Learned: Managed UEM

1196. How actively and meaningfully were stakeholders involved in the Managed UEM project?

1197. What solutions or recommendations can you offer that would have improved some aspect of the Managed UEM project?

1198. How did the estimated Managed UEM project Budget compare with the total actual expenditures?

1199. What would you approach differently next time?

1200. To what extent was the evolution of risks communicated?

1201. Where do you go from here?

1202. What is your overall assessment of the outcome of this Managed UEM project?

1203. Was there enough support – guidance, clerical support, training?

1204. How effectively were issues managed on the Managed UEM project?

1205. Do you have any real problems?

1206. How extensive is middle management?

1207. How well were expectations met regarding the frequency and content of information that was conveyed to by the Managed UEM project Manager?

1208. What if anything has been lacking?

1209. What were the key issues?

1210. How effectively and consistently was sponsorship for the Managed UEM project conveyed?

1211. What are your lessons learned that you will keep in mind for the next Managed UEM project you participate in?

1212. What is the desired end-state?

1213. What was helpful to know when planning the deployment?

1214. What were the major enablers to a quick response?

1215. How well was Managed UEM project status communicated throughout your involvement in the Managed UEM project?

Index

engagement 50, 129, 193, 205, 234
Engineers 147
enhance 90, 238
enhanced 111
enhancing 95
enlarged 201
enough 7, 68, 105, 110, 112, 125, 143, 209, 259
ensure 38, 43, 63, 65, 80, 102, 108, 118, 121, 133, 146, 150, 167, 175, 183, 185, 189, 229-230, 253
ensuring 10, 118, 133, 224, 242-243
entails 224
Enterprise 215
entire 183
entities 54
entity 1
equipment 17, 26, 182, 209, 244-245, 252
equipped 31
equitably 35, 228, 230
equivalent 209
errors 104, 125, 182
especially 168
essential 81, 176, 230
essentials 116
establish 73, 96, 178
estimate 45, 52, 56, 169, 248
-estimate 179
estimated 41, 43, 53, 56, 109, 177, 246, 259
estimates 3-4, 35, 57, 65, 137, 154, 167, 175, 180, 206
estimating 4, 137, 154, 169, 175, 177-178
estimation 79, 132, 192
estimators 175
etcetera 52, 123
ethical 109, 249
ethnic 115
evaluate 77, 131, 181
evaluated 180, 207-208, 253
evaluating 86, 167
evaluation 66, 75-76, 97, 135, 184, 207-208, 232, 236, 252
events 26, 73, 76, 78, 151
everyday 59
everyone 35, 37, 183, 185
everything 46
evidence 13, 53, 183, 198, 215, 232

statements   13, 27, 30, 41, 43, 57, 65, 72, 87, 100, 123, 139, 145, 185
status 5-6, 62, 137-138, 144, 153, 191, 215, 234, 242, 246, 260
steady 54
steering   146, 192, 205
storage   217, 224, 238
stored 138, 232
stories 32
strategic   54, 89, 106, 182, 206, 209
strategies   90, 104, 122, 221-222
strategy   19, 37, 45, 75, 78, 80, 95, 107, 111, 118, 120, 133, 136, 175, 191, 194, 206, 212
Stream 64, 71
strengths   136, 160, 248
stretch 113
strict   72
strive   113
strong 190
Strongly   12, 17, 28, 44, 58, 73, 88, 101
structure   3, 52, 108, 118, 132, 144, 148, 165, 199, 201
structured   122, 191
structures   239, 241
stubborn   107
stupid 114
styles   182
subfactor   207
subject9-10, 42
Subjective   184
subjects   67
submit 11, 217
submitted   11, 219-220
subsequent   208
subset 19
succeed   46, 112, 160
success   22, 25, 29, 32, 37, 40, 47, 49-50, 53, 76, 84-85, 88, 111-113, 120, 123, 145-146, 154, 161, 191, 199, 206, 213, 215, 230
successes   107
successful   58, 80, 99, 109, 111, 165-166, 179, 215, 234
succession   95, 130
suffered   230
sufficient   199, 201, 217, 237
suggested   97, 219
suitable   151, 195, 200

CPSIA information can be obtained
at www.ICGtesting.com
Printed in the USA
BVHW042306280719
554530BV00014B/959/P

9 780655 820192